COOK WHEN YOU CAN

EAT WHEN YOU WANT

COOK WHEN YOU CAN

EAT WHEN YOU WANT

PREP ONCE
for Delicious
Meals All Week

CAROLINE PESSIN

PHOTOGRAPHY BY
CHARLY DESLANDES

BLACK DOG
& LEVENTHAL
PUBLISHERS
NEW YORK

PREFACE

If, like me, you are a fan of all things homemade, and you try to avoid all commercially made foods, but at the same time your workdays are so full you have neither the time nor the energy during the week to cook . . .

If, like me, you try to offer your family healthy and balanced meals that appeal to both adults and kids . . .

If, like me, you find that ordering takeout or delivery leaves a large hole in your food budget . . .

And, if the question "What's for dinner?" each night from your family has become your weekly obsession . . . then you will love the cooking method presented in this book, a method often referred to as "batch cooking" or "the meal-prep method," consisting of preparing meals in advance for every night of the week!

Ever since I discovered this method, I save money and eat a balanced diet, all while freeing up my weeknights to enjoy more time with my family and eliminating the stress caused from having to plan and prepare a meal each night.

On weekends, this method takes about 2 hours of my time to peel, cut, marinate, and cook several dishes at once. Then, during the week, I just either reheat, assemble, or finish the meal with some quick final steps—and dinner is ready!

Several of my friends have tried this approach and they love it. And I'm convinced once you try it, you'll love it, too!

INTRODUCTION

What a joy it is to come home each night from work without the worry of deciding what to make for dinner! Nothing offers more peace of mind during the week than knowing you will have to spend very little time cooking at the end of the day, and that you will get to enjoy a delicious and balanced meal that requires minimal cleanup.

These questions each night are familiar to many of us: "What am I going to make for dinner?" "Do I have what I need in the fridge?" "How will I be able to cook a delicious and healthy meal and spend time with the kids, give them their baths, help them with homework, etc.?"

When we feel overwhelmed with the answers to these questions, we often end up giving in to what's easiest: just boiling some pasta, or heating a frozen prepackaged dinner, or opting for delivery—all of which are less healthy and less economical choices!

But by adopting a different approach to organizing your meals and cooking, it is possible to alleviate the stress of making dinner each night for your family.

The idea is simple: during the weekend, set aside about 2 hours all at once for cooking an entire week's worth of meals.

In this book, we have laid out for you 16 varied and balanced menus, grouped by the seasons. The menus are designed to feed a family of 4, with enough in quantity to feed 2 adults and 2 teenagers. If you have small children, or if you are only 3 people, you can take the leftovers to the office the next day to enjoy as lunch.

Each menu has 7 recipes: 5 entrées and 2 appetizers (for evenings when the entrées are lighter). We chose not to include desserts because most of us simply eat a piece of fruit or perhaps some ice cream after dinner; and many of us like to leave our sweeter indulgences for the weekends.

With this method, Monday to Friday, you no longer have to worry about what to make for dinner or have to do last-minute shopping, and you will spend 30 minutes or less in the kitchen each night—that's a promise!

TO ACCOMPLISH THIS METHOD OF COOKING, SIMPLY FOLLOW THESE STEPS:

1. Choose one of the seasonal menus that appeals to you.

2. Do your food shopping on the weekend (Friday night, Saturday, or Sunday). Each menu's ingredients are very common and can be found easily in typical supermarkets. Only in a very few cases will it be necessary to make a quick side trip to a specialty food store or market.

3. Choose a weekend day, Saturday or Sunday, where you have a free block of 2 hours in front of you. It is best to cook on Sunday, however, rather than Saturday, to ensure everything stays its freshest throughout the week and to cut down on the number of meals you have to freeze.

4. Before you begin cooking, set out all the listed ingredients on your countertop or work surface. This is a tip for saving even more time because it avoids trips to the refrigerator or pantry each time you need something.

5. Before you begin cooking, set out all the necessary equipment and utensils that are listed. If you do this, you will have everything at your fingertips while you cook.

6. Follow the steps of the recipes as they are written, as they were developed according to actual preparation times.

7. Store the finished dishes and ingredients as instructed at the end of each cooking session. In general, dishes to be served Monday to Wednesday can be refrigerated, while those to be served Thursday and Friday should be frozen.

The result? During each night of the week, all you have to do is follow the instructions for assembling, reheating, or completing the meals with some quick, final steps. In all, you will spend less than half an hour in your kitchen each night. Some nights, there is nothing to do except reheat an entrée. Other nights you'll need to do some last-minute cooking, some quick final prep, or just combine some ingredients.

WHAT ARE THE ADVANTAGES OF THIS METHOD?

First, this method offers an undeniable peace of mind during the week by eliminating the hassle of deciding what to prepare for dinner as well as eliminating the need to do last-minute shopping at the end of the day.

Second, this method is a real time-saver because not only will you spend much less time cooking, you will also spend less time washing and putting away the dishes. Use the extra time you gain each night by resting, or spending time with your family.

Third, this method offers a variety of balanced meals with delicious homemade flavors without all the additives and preservatives you find in some commercially produced or restaurant-prepared meals.

And finally, this method offers considerable savings for your food budget because there are fewer pricey home-delivery meals as well as less waste, as we have created these menus to use up each ingredient entirely by the end of the week—it's a "zero waste" kitchen!

WHAT ARE THE DISADVANTAGES OF THIS METHOD?

Spending 2 hours cooking on a single day can be a bit tiring. You may feel you are wasting part of your weekend, which often already seems too short. But you will see that the relaxation provided by this method during the week makes these 2 hours well worth it. In addition, we have done everything to make the cooking sessions easy: the preparation is provided step by step, and the photos allow you to see what the finished dishes should look like.

WHAT EQUIPMENT DO I NEED?

The menus can be accomplished in any average kitchen equipped with an oven with at least 2 racks and a cooktop with at least 3 burners. During the cooking session, all the cooking is done simultaneously, which again offers a savings of time as well as energy costs for running the stove and ovens.

For the equipment and containers needed for preparing the menus, see page XII.

BEFORE YOU START:

* Make room in your freezer. Maybe plan some "empty-the-freezer" meals beforehand to free up freezer space.
* Before leaving for the supermarket, sort through your refrigerator, discard any stale or questionable foods, clean the shelves with white vinegar to remove odors and bacteria, and consume any leftovers you find.

We challenge you to test this method with at least one menu and see the positive change it has on your weeknights. You may not stop after just one menu but quickly adopt this method for every week!

REFRIGERATION

EXPECTED SHELF LIFE:

1 WEEK:
* Washed lettuce
* Washed herbs
* Cut vegetables
* Chopped onions and garlic
* Vinaigrette

5 DAYS:
* Hard-boiled eggs
* Hummus
* Home-cooked legumes
  (lentils, chickpeas, dried beans, etc.)

3 TO 4 DAYS:
* Cooked grains (rice, quinoa)
* Cooked vegetables
* Broth- and cream-based soups, gazpachos
* Meatless gratins

2 DAYS:
* Marinated meats
* Cooked fish and meats
* Quiche, flaky pastries

TIPS:
* Do not prepare potatoes until the last minute: When sliced and kept raw they will oxidize, and when cooked in advance they will take on a bad flavor.
* For grains that cook quickly (rice, pasta, couscous), be sure to cook them at the last minute for the best flavor and optimal texture.
* Store stewed dishes and soups in the pans or pots in which they were prepared so that you can easily reheat them.
* Frozen homemade dishes should be consumed within 2 months for a texture that is the least altered.

ESSENTIAL EQUIPMENT

FOR COOKING:

For the menus in this book, make sure you have the following cookware on hand:

* 1 lidded Dutch oven or stockpot (even better if you have both)
* 1 sauté pan
* 1 skillet
* 3 saucepans of different sizes
* Optional: 1 wok, 1 steam cooker

The equipment needed for these menus is very basic, requiring no professional-level tools at all: mixing bowls, ramekins, colander, strainer, sheet pan, gratin baking dish or shallow baking dish, tart pan, round cake pan, loaf pan, salad spinner, immersion blender, food mill (or potato masher), small food processor, zester or grater, and a skimmer.

FOR STORING:

This book is unique because it requires foods and prepared entrées to be stored. It is essential, therefore, that you have several airtight containers on hand. Choose glass containers, which are more hygienic than plastic and can be placed safely in the oven or microwave. You will find many of these types of containers at large retailers and home stores at very reasonable prices.

You will need a maximum of:

* 1 very large container for storing salads
* 3 large containers
* 5 medium containers
* 3 small containers
* 2 small airtight containers for storing chopped onions and garlic, to seal off odors
* 1 (6-cup/1.5-L-capacity) glass jar for storing soups and gazpachos

Also, be sure to keep in your pantry: plastic wrap, freezer bags, and paper towels.

STAPLES

The following ingredients are used frequently in the menus, so be sure to keep these stocked:

* Quick-cooking grains (such as durum wheat, lentils, etc.)
* Dried bread crumbs
* Tomato sauce
* Basic spices: cloves, herbes de Provence, cinnamon, curry, ground cumin, dried thyme, ras el hanout spice blend, whole nutmeg, and bay leaves
* All-purpose flour*
* Sunflower oil
* Olive oil
* Ketchup
* Lentils
* Baking powder

* Cornstarch
* Honey
* Mustard
* Dried pasta
* Black pepper
* Quinoa
* White rice
* Brown rice
* Couscous
* Soy sauce
* Table salt, sea salt (preferably gray and fleur de sel)
* Balsamic vinegar
* Wine vinegar

For those allergic to gluten, you can use gluten-free pasta and flour.

SPRING MENUS

SPRING MENU #1

MONDAY
Garlic leg of lamb, roasted spring vegetables, white kidney beans

TUESDAY
Appetizer: Asparagus velouté soup

Main: Herb-crusted fresh cod

WEDNESDAY
Shepherd's pie

THURSDAY
Appetizer: White-bean hummus, vegetable sticks

Main: Asparagus and fresh cod pasta

FRIDAY
Minestrone

SPRING MENU #2

MONDAY
Salmon and watercress pie

TUESDAY
Appetizer: Radish toasts

Main: Tarragon chicken

WEDNESDAY
Lentil dal

THURSDAY
Appetizer: Creamy radish-greens spread

Main: Caesar salad

FRIDAY
Green curry monkfish

SPRING MENU #3 page 31

MONDAY
Appetizer: Fennel marinated in olive oil and lemon

Main: Turkey cordon bleu*

TUESDAY
Marinated hanger steak, puréed baby carrots

WEDNESDAY
Spinach and ricotta–stuffed shells

THURSDAY
Niçoise salad

FRIDAY
Appetizer: Warm goat cheese toasts

Main: Shrimp pad thai

*For a pork-free menu, replace the ham with sliced cooked turkey breast.

SPRING MENU #4 page 45

MONDAY
Veal chop with spring vegetables

TUESDAY
Appetizer: Cauliflower in caper vinaigrette

Main: Savory cheesecake

WEDNESDAY
Appetizer: Smoked mackerel rillettes

Main: Chicken puttanesca and rice

THURSDAY
Spiced bulgur with cauliflower, broccoli, and chickpeas

FRIDAY
Smoked mackerel tagliatelle and vegetables

SUMMER MENUS

SUMMER MENU #1 page 61

MONDAY
Appetizer: Quinoa tabbouleh
Main: Chicken thighs and ratatouille

TUESDAY
Prosciutto di Parma* and vegetable pizza

WEDNESDAY
Zucchini, olive, and chicken pasta

THURSDAY
Appetizer: Goat cheese and ratatouille turnovers
Main: Stuffed tomatoes and rice

FRIDAY
Family-size vegetable pasta salad

*For a pork-free menu, replace the prosciutto with sliced cooked turkey breast.

SUMMER MENU #2 page 75

MONDAY
Family-size potato, salmon, mesclun, onion, and cucumber salad

TUESDAY
Appetizer: Greek lentil salad
Main: Stuffed zucchini

WEDNESDAY
Moussaka

THURSDAY
Fish blanquette with dill and rice

FRIDAY
Appetizer: Pea, feta, and mint soup
Main: Lentil meatballs in tomato sauce with string beans

SUMMER MENU #3 page 89

MONDAY
Marinated chicken kebabs, durum wheat with roasted vegetables

TUESDAY
Merguez sausage, couscous

WEDNESDAY
Appetizer: Eggplant caviar

Main: Spanish omelet

THURSDAY
Summer bruschetta

FRIDAY
Appetizer: Bell peppers marinated in garlic and olive oil

Main: Tunisian spaghetti

SUMMER MENU #4 page 103

MONDAY
Appetizer: Zucchini gazpacho

Main: Tuna and tomato quiche

TUESDAY
Shrimp and pineapple fried rice

WEDNESDAY
Appetizer: Tzatziki sauce

Main: Zucchini and ham loaf*

THURSDAY
Chickpea burgers

FRIDAY
Farfalle and smoked salmon salad

*For a pork-free menu, replace the ham with sliced cooked turkey breast.

FALL MENUS

FALL MENU #1
page 119

MONDAY
Pasta with beef cheek sauce

TUESDAY
Appetizer: Hummus with dipping vegetables and pita bread
Main: Butternut-chestnut soup with lardons*

WEDNESDAY
Appetizer: Field lettuce, green apple, and cashew salad
Main: Shepherd's pie

THURSDAY
Butternut squash and spinach fried rice, toasted cashews

FRIDAY
Pho

*For a pork-free menu, replace the lardons with smoked tofu.

FALL MENU #2
page 133

MONDAY
Appetizer: Cauliflower velouté soup with sautéed shrimp
Main: Polenta pizza with mushrooms

TUESDAY
Sweet potato* and chicken curry

WEDNESDAY
Cauliflower and potato gratin with ham**

THURSDAY
Appetizer: Cabbage, boiled egg, and cherry tomato salad with creamy dressing
Main: Linguine with garlic cream, arugula, walnuts, and Parmesan shavings

FRIDAY
Fresh cod and sweet potato* shepherd's pie

*If you do not like sweet potatoes, replace half the quantity with carrots (for the curry) and the other half with potatoes (for the cod shepherd's pie), following the instructions exactly as written.
**For a pork-free menu, replace the ham with turkey breast.

FALL MENU #3 page 147

MONDAY

Appetizer: Tuna rillettes endive bites

Main: Turnip, honey, and goat cheese tart Tatin

TUESDAY

Lamb tagine with quince

WEDNESDAY

Appetizer: Spinach and *fromage frais* velouté soup

Main: Potato, leek, onion, and lardons gratin*

THURSDAY

Lamb keftas, panfried carrots, turnips, and chickpeas with cumin

FRIDAY

Salmon and spinach lasagna

*For a pork-free menu, replace the lardons with smoked tofu.

FALL MENU #4 page 161

MONDAY

Appetizer: Cherry tomatoes, Parmesan, squash seeds, and thyme in flaky pastry

Main: Vegetarian chili

TUESDAY

Pumpkin and chicken couscous

WEDNESDAY

Ham* and broccoli noodle bake

THURSDAY

Chicken and vegetable crumble

FRIDAY

Appetizer: Pumpkin curry velouté soup

Main: Pollack in shallot sauce, steamed potatoes

*For a pork-free menu, replace the ham with turkey breast.

WINTER MENUS

WINTER MENU #1 page 177

MONDAY
Appetizer: Leeks in vinaigrette with deviled eggs
Main: Orzo pasta in beef broth

TUESDAY
Pot-au-feu

WEDNESDAY
Appetizer: Beef and vegetable samosas
Main: Haddock brandade

THURSDAY
Vegetable velouté soup, marrow toasts

FRIDAY
Haddock and coconut milk soup

WINTER MENU #2 page 191

MONDAY
Quiche lorraine*

TUESDAY
Appetizer: Leek and potato velouté soup
Main: Caramelized chicken wings

WEDNESDAY
Appetizer: Red cabbage, grape, and apple salad
Main: Slow-cooked veal and chorizo* stew

THURSDAY
Cream of lentils, mushrooms, and carrots

FRIDAY
Spicy veal blanquette

*For a pork-free menu, replace the lardons in the quiche with diced turkey meat, and the chorizo with a pinch of chile pepper.

WINTER MENU #3 page 205

MONDAY

Appetizer: Celery root and parsnip velouté soup with scallops

Main: Crustless goat cheese and broccoli quiche

TUESDAY

Duck breast à l'orange, scalloped potatoes

WEDNESDAY

Appetizer: Chickpea and orange salad

Main: Roasted red kuri squash, quinoa, goat cheese, hazelnuts

THURSDAY

Duck and noodles Chinese stir-fry

FRIDAY

Scallop spaghetti

WINTER MENU #4 page 219

MONDAY

Salt pork in lentils

TUESDAY

Tartiflette and crudités

WEDNESDAY

Appetizer: Stuffed brioche buns

Main: Whiting fish meatballs with winter vegetables

THURSDAY

Appetizer: Warm lentil salad, gribiche sauce

Main: Beef tenderloin, Roquefort cheese sauce

FRIDAY

Croque monsieur

SPRING

MENU #1

SHOPPING LIST MENU #1

FRUITS / VEGETABLES

* 1 bunch carrots
* 12 spears green asparagus
* 8 small turnips
* 4 clusters cherry tomatoes
* 3⅓ lb (1.5 kg) Charlotte potatoes
* 1 small lemon
* 1 bunch green onions
* 1 bunch parsley
* 1 bunch basil
* 6 cloves garlic

PANTRY AND STAPLES

* All-purpose flour
* Olive oil
* Salt, pepper

MEAT / FISH

* 2¼ lb (1 kg) leg of lamb
* 1¾ lb (800 g) fresh cod (strips from the back)

COLD CASE

* 2 tbsp (5 g) grated Parmesan cheese
* 1⅓ cups (320 mL) cream
* 3½ tbsp (50 g) unsalted butter

DRY AND CANNED GOODS

* 2 cans white kidney beans
  (1⅔ lb/500 g drained, liquid reserved)
* 14 oz (400 g) short pasta
* 7 tbsp (50 g) pine nuts
* Tahini (optional)
* Ground cumin
* Dried bread crumbs

MENUS

MONDAY

Garlic leg of lamb, roasted spring vegetables, white kidney beans

TUESDAY

Appetizer: Asparagus velouté soup

Main: Herb-crusted fresh cod

WEDNESDAY

Shepherd's pie

THURSDAY

Appetizer: White-bean hummus, vegetable sticks

Main: Asparagus and fresh cod pasta

FRIDAY

Minestrone

SET UP

If you have enough work space, set out all the ingredients needed for this cooking session. This includes everything except 3 clusters of the cherry tomatoes, the pasta, and the bread crumbs. Doing this will allow you to have everything at your fingertips and to not lose time searching for the ingredients in the pantry or refrigerator.

SET OUT THE NECESSARY EQUIPMENT:

* 2 large baking dishes
* 1 gratin baking dish or shallow baking dish
* 1 food mill (or potato masher)
* 1 sauté pan
* 1 large saucepan
* 1 medium saucepan
* 1 immersion blender
* 1 food processor
* 1 (6-cup/1.5-L-capacity) glass jar (for storing the asparagus velouté soup)
* 3 containers: 2 medium + 1 large
* Plastic wrap

EVERYTHING IS NOW READY FOR A COOKING TIME OF 1 HOUR AND 45 MINUTES!

1. Preheat the oven to 350°F (180°C). Peel the garlic cloves, cut them in half, and remove any green sprout from the centers. Place the leg of lamb in a large baking dish. Make six deep incisions in the lamb using a knife. Insert a garlic clove half into each incision. Season the lamb with salt and pepper, then rub it all over with pieces of the butter. Bake for 40 minutes.

2. Bring two saucepans of salted water to a boil: one large and one medium. Peel the potatoes, turnips, and asparagus. Cut the potatoes in half crosswise, place them in the large saucepan of boiling water, and cook for 20 minutes. Quarter 2 of the turnips. Cut 2 of the turnips into sticks. Leave the 4 remaining turnips whole. Place the turnip quarters and the asparagus in the medium saucepan of boiling water, and cook for 10 minutes.

3. Cut off and discard the root ends of the green onions. Chop the onions, and add half of them to the saucepan with the turnips and asparagus. Add 1 garlic clove half to the saucepan.

4. Peel the carrots. Leave 6 of the carrots whole. Cut half the remaining carrots into rounds and the other half into sticks. Place the carrot sticks in a medium-size container. Add the turnip sticks to the container; the raw vegetable sticks will be used for dipping in the hummus.

5. Remove 6 asparagus spears from the saucepan. Rinse them under cold water to maintain their color, then cut them into pieces. Set them aside in a medium-size container.

6. Drain the water from the saucepan containing the remaining asparagus. Add half the cream, ½ tsp of salt, a little pepper, and 2 of the cooked potatoes. Blend using an immersion blender until smooth. Transfer the mixture to a jar.

7. When the lamb has cooked for 40 minutes, add the 4 whole turnips, the whole carrots, 1 cluster

of the cherry tomatoes, and ¾ cup (200 g) of the beans with their liquid to the baking dish. Season with salt and pepper, and let cook for another 20 minutes.

8. Wash and gently dry the parsley and basil.

9. Prepare the herb crust for the cod. In a food processor, place 4 tbsp (30 g) of pine nuts, ¼ cup (30 g) of flour, half the parsley, half the basil, a garlic clove half, and a little salt and pepper. Process to form a paste. Spread the paste over the cod strips. Place the cod in a baking dish, and bake for 15 minutes.

10. In the sauté pan, heat 1 tbsp (15 mL) of olive oil. Add the remaining chopped onions, sliced carrots, and ½ tsp of salt. Let cook for 5 minutes, or until softened. Add 2 cups (480 mL) of water, and let cook for another 10 minutes.

11. Meanwhile, make the pesto: In the food processor used to make the herb crust (there is no need to wash it), place the remaining 3 tbsp (20 g) of pine nuts, 2 garlic clove halves, the remaining basil,

half the Parmesan, ½ tsp of salt, and 1 pinch of pepper. Pulse to combine while slowly adding 1 tbsp (15 mL) of olive oil.

12. Dice 2 of the potatoes. Add the diced potatoes to the sauté pan along with 1 cup (150 g) of the beans. Off the heat, add the pesto. Stir to combine, then transfer the minestrone to a large container.

13. Purée the remaining potatoes using a food mill (or potato masher), then combine them with the remaining cream, ½ tsp of salt, and 1 pinch of pepper.

14. Bone the leg of lamb and cut it into 6 slices. In a food processor or using an immersion blender, process the two least attractive pieces together with 2 tbsp (8 g) of parsley, 2 cooked carrots, and a little of the cooking juices. Place the mixture in a baking dish, and cover it with the puréed potatoes.

15. Make the white-bean hummus: In a clean food processor, place the remaining beans (drained), the remaining garlic, 1 tsp (5 g) of tahini, if using,

the juice of the lemon, and 1 pinch of cumin. Process until smooth. Transfer the mixture to an attractive serving bowl. Sprinkle half the remaining chopped parsley on top. Sprinkle the remaining chopped parsley on top of the leg of lamb.

16. Crumble one-fourth of the cooked herb-crusted cod. Add the crumbled cod to the container with the asparagus.

IT'S ALL DONE! LET COOL.

PLACE IN THE REFRIGERATOR:

* The leg of lamb and the accompanying vegetables, directly in the serving dish, covered with plastic wrap (keeps for 2 days)

* The asparagus velouté soup (keeps for 3 days)

* The herb-crusted cod, if you are serving it within 2 days of preparing it

* The white-bean hummus, covered with plastic wrap (keeps for 5 days)

* The vegetable sticks (keeps for 1 week)

PLACE IN THE FREEZER:

* The herb-crusted cod, if you are serving it more than two days after preparing it
* The shepherd's pie, in its serving dish, covered with plastic wrap
* The container with the asparagus pieces and cod
* The minestrone

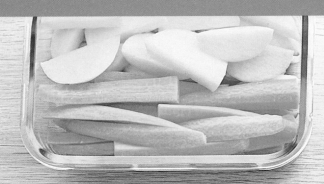

EACH NIGHT'S PREP

MONDAY

Main: Garlic leg of lamb, roasted spring vegetables, white kidney beans

Reheating time: 10 minutes

Ingredients: garlic leg of lamb, roasted spring vegetables, white kidney beans

Preheat the oven to 350°F (180°C), and reheat the leg of lamb and the accompanying vegetables for 10 minutes.

For Tuesday, if you have frozen the herb-crusted cod, remove it from the freezer and place it in the refrigerator to thaw.

TUESDAY

Appetizer: Asparagus velouté soup

Main: Herb-crusted fresh cod

Cooking and reheating time: 10 minutes

Ingredients: the asparagus velouté soup, the herb-crusted cod, 2 clusters of cherry tomatoes, olive oil

In a saucepan, reheat the soup for 10 minutes. Preheat the oven to 400°F (200°C). Roast the cherry tomatoes for 7 minutes with a drizzle of olive oil. Lower the temperature of the oven to 300°F (150°C), and add the cod, and reheat for 3 minutes.

For Wednesday, remove the shepherd's pie from the freezer and place it in the refrigerator to thaw.

WEDNESDAY

Main: Shepherd's pie

Reheating time: 10 minutes

Ingredients: the shepherd's pie, a little of the dried bread crumbs

Preheat the oven to 400°F (200°C). Sprinkle the top of the shepherd's pie with the bread crumbs and bake for 10 minutes.

For Thursday, remove the container of asparagus and cod from the freezer and place it in the refrigerator to thaw.

THURSDAY

Appetizer: White-bean hummus, vegetable sticks

Main: Asparagus and fresh cod pasta

Cooking and reheating time: 15 minutes

Preparation time: 1 minute

Ingredients: the raw vegetable sticks, the hummus, the pasta, the container with the asparagus pieces and cod, and the remaining Parmesan

Cook the pasta according to the directions on the package. Set aside one-third of the pasta for Friday's minestrone in a container in the refrigerator. Reheat the asparagus and the cod in the microwave. Add them to the remaining pasta and stir briefly to combine. Sprinkle with the Parmesan.

For Friday, remove the minestrone from the freezer and place it in the refrigerator to thaw.

FRIDAY

Main: Minestrone

Reheating time: 10 minutes

Ingredients: the remaining cooked pasta, the minestrone, 1 cluster of cherry tomatoes

Reheat the minestrone in a large saucepan with the cherry tomatoes for 10 minutes. Add the cooked pasta, and serve.

MENU #2

SHOPPING LIST   MENU #2

FRUITS / VEGETABLES

* 2 bunches watercress
* 1 large bag (about 9 oz/250 g) baby spinach (sell-by date > 4 days)
* 1 bunch radishes
* 1 bunch green onions
* 3 heads romaine lettuce
* 1 large potato
* 1 organic lime
* 1 lemon
* 1 bunch cilantro
* 1 bunch tarragon
* 3 shallots
* 8 garlic cloves
* 1 (2-in./5-cm) knob fresh ginger

PANTRY AND STAPLES

* 1 cup (7 oz/200 g) red lentils
* 2¾ cups (18 oz/500 g) microwaveable pouch of quick-cooking white rice
* Just over ¾ cup (200 mL) tomato sauce
* Mustard
* Olive oil
* Salt, black pepper

MEAT / FISH

* 1 (7-oz/200-g) salmon fillet
* 1 monkfish tail (ask your fishmonger to skin the fish and cut the tail into cubes)
* 8 small boneless, skinless chicken breasts

COLD CASE

* 4 large eggs
* 1 small wedge Parmesan cheese
* 1 cup (9 oz/250 g) mascarpone cheese
* 1 cup (9 oz/250 g) ricotta cheese
* 2 cups (16 oz/454 g) crème fraîche or plain yogurt
* 1⅓ cups (320 mL) heavy cream
* 2 (9-in./23-cm) piecrusts

DRY AND CANNED GOODS

* 1 large loaf whole-grain bread
* 1⅔ cups (400 mL) coconut milk
* ⅔ tsp (⅓ oz/10 g) green curry paste
* 2 cardamom pods
* 1 tbsp (¼ oz/7 g) tandoori spice blend
* 8 anchovies
* Worcestershire sauce
* Tabasco sauce

MENUS

MONDAY
Salmon and watercress pie

TUESDAY
Appetizer: Radish toasts

Main: Tarragon chicken

WEDNESDAY
Lentil dal

THURSDAY
Appetizer: Creamy radish-greens spread

Main: Caesar salad

FRIDAY
Green curry monkfish

SET UP

If you have enough work space, set out all the ingredients needed for this cooking session. This includes everything except the baby spinach, romaine, 1 garlic clove, chicken, cream, Parmesan, rice, Worcestershire sauce, Tabasco sauce, and anchovies. This allows you to have everything at your fingertips and to not lose time searching for the ingredients in the pantry or refrigerator.

SET OUT THE NECESSARY EQUIPMENT:

* 1 food processor
* 1 salad spinner (or large bowl and clean kitchen towel)
* 1 skillet
* 1 (8-in./20-cm) round cake pan
* 1 sauté pan
* 1 immersion blender
* 1 small saucepan
* 1 large saucepan
* 1 small grater (for the lime zest and fresh ginger)

* 1 small ovenproof bowl
* 1 (6-cup/1.5-L-capacity) glass jar (for storing the radish-greens spread)
* 7 containers: 2 large + 1 medium + 4 small
* 1 airtight storage bag, paper towels, plastic wrap

EVERYTHING IS NOW READY FOR A COOKING TIME OF 2 HOURS!

1. Cut off and discard the stems from the watercress. Wash and dry the leaves using the salad spinner (or fill a large bowl with water and wash the leaves, then gently pat them dry with the kitchen towel), then roughly chop them. Set aside 1 handful of the chopped leaves in a bowl.

2. Peel and chop the shallots and 7 of the garlic cloves.

3. In the skillet over medium-high heat, heat 1 tbsp (15 mL) of olive oil until warm. Add one-third of the shallots, ½ tsp of the chopped garlic, and ½ tsp of salt. Cook for 2 minutes, or until softened.

Add the chopped watercress leaves (except what was set aside in the bowl), and cook for 5 more minutes over high heat, or until the liquid has evaporated.

4. Meanwhile, fill the small saucepan with water, bring it to a boil, and cook 1 egg for 10 minutes.

5. Break the remaining 3 eggs into a bowl. Set aside half a raw egg yolk (it will be used to brush the piecrust). In the food processor, place the raw eggs, mascarpone, ½ tsp of salt, and a little pepper. Pulse to combine. Add the cooked watercress mixture and pulse again to combine.

6. Preheat the oven to 350°F (180°C). Cut the salmon into small cubes and add them to the food processor. Grease the cake pan and line it with one of the piecrusts. Fold and gently press any excess dough down onto the interior sides of the pan. Cut out a circle from the second piecrust the same diameter as the pan. Scrape the watercress-salmon mixture into the dough-lined cake pan, then place the dough circle on top. Tuck the excess dough

down into the pan along the edges, and brush the crust with the reserved half egg yolk. Using a knife, cut a small hole in the center of the dough, then roll up a small piece of parchment paper and stick it into the hole to create a little "chimney." Bake for 50 minutes, or until golden and flaky on top.

7. Cut off the radish greens level with the tops of the radishes. Place the greens in the salad spinner and gently wash them several times (or in a large bowl with fresh water). Wash the radishes, cut them into rounds, then place them in a small container.

8. In the large saucepan over very low heat, heat 1 tbsp (15 mL) of olive oil until warm. Add half the remaining chopped shallots, ½ tsp of chopped garlic, and ½ tsp of salt. Let cook for 5 minutes, until softened. Meanwhile, peel the potato and cut it into small dice. Add the diced potato to the saucepan, then add 1⅔ cups (400 mL) of water. Let cook for 10 minutes.

9. Rinse and finely chop the green onions. Wash and gently dry the cilantro and tarragon. Peel the ginger.

10. To the large saucepan with the potatoes, add the radish greens, the reserved watercress, 1 sprig of tarragon, and 1 tbsp of the chopped green portion of the onions. Cook for 3 minutes. Add 3 tbsp (1¾ oz/50 g) of the ricotta cheese, then blend using the immersion blender. Transfer the mixture to the glass jar, leaving a little room at the top.

11. In the food processor, place 2 tbsp of chopped green onions, 1 tsp of chopped garlic, one-third of the cilantro with the stems, half the ginger, and all of the green curry paste. Process until smooth.

12. Prepare the green curry monkfish: In the sauté pan over high heat, bring half the coconut milk to a boil and let it reduce by half. Stir in the green curry mixture, and let boil for 1 minute. Add the monkfish cubes, and let cook, uncovered, for 5 minutes. At the end of the cooking time, grate the lime zest into the pan, then add the

juice of half the lemon. Transfer the mixture to the medium-size container. Rinse and wipe out the pan.

13. Prepare the lentil dal: Grate the remaining ginger. In the sauté pan over medium-high heat, heat 1 tbsp (15 mL) of olive oil until warm. Add half the remaining chopped garlic and shallots, 1 tsp of salt, the tandoori spice blend, the cardamom pods, and the grated ginger. Let cook for 1 minute, then add the lentils, tomato sauce, and 1¼ cups (300 mL) of water. Let simmer for 15 minutes over low heat. If the dal becomes too thick, add a little more water during the cooking time.

14. Slice 8 attractive slices of bread and set them aside. Cut the remaining bread (the two heels) into cubes. Place the bread cubes in a small ovenproof bowl with 2 tbsp (30 mL) of olive oil, ½ tsp of salt, and half the remaining garlic. Stir to combine, then bake at 350°F (180°C) for 10 minutes, or until the bread cubes are golden. Place the croutons in a small container.

* The remaining chopped green onions (keeps for 1 week)
* The radish slices (keeps for 1 week)
* The tarragon sauce (keeps for 3 days)
* The remaining cilantro and tarragon, in an airtight container between two sheets of paper towels (keeps for 1 week)
* The 8 slices of bread, in the airtight storage bag (keeps for 4 days)

PLACE IN THE FREEZER:

* The green curry monkfish
* The creamy radish-greens spread

PANTRY:

* The croutons

15. Once the lentils are tender, add the remaining coconut milk and the juice of the lime. Stir to combine for 1 minute on the heat.

16. Prepare the tarragon sauce: In the small saucepan, heat 1 tsp (5 mL) of olive oil until warm. Add the remaining garlic and shallots, then add ½ tsp of salt, and let cook for 3 minutes, or until slightly softened. Add 2 tbsp (30 g) of mustard, the crème fraîche, and three-fourths of the tarragon. Bring to a boil, let cook for 2 minutes, then remove the pan from the heat and blend using the immersion blender.

IT'S ALL DONE! LET COOL.

PLACE IN THE REFRIGERATOR:

* The hard-boiled egg (keeps for 5 days)
* The salmon and watercress pie, in its pan (keeps for 2 days)
* The lentil dal (keeps for 4 days)

EACH NIGHT'S PREP

MONDAY

Main: Salmon and watercress pie

Reheating time: 10 minutes

Ingredients: the salmon and watercress pie

Preheat the oven to 350°F (180°C). Reheat the pie for 10 minutes.

TUESDAY

Appetizer: Radish toasts

Main: Tarragon chicken

Cooking time: 15 minutes

Preparation time: 10 minutes

Ingredients: the 8 slices of bread, the remaining ricotta cheese, the radish slices, the chopped green onions, olive oil, chicken breasts, the tarragon sauce, the remaining tarragon, salt, and pepper

Toast the slices of bread. Spread some of the ricotta cheese on top of each slice, then top with a few radish slices, green onions, and salt and pepper. Set aside several of the radish slices for Thursday. Chop the tarragon.

In a large skillet over medium-high heat, heat 2 tbsp (30 mL) of olive oil until warm, and cook the chicken breasts for 15 minutes, or until cooked through. Remove 4 of the chicken breasts, and refrigerate in an airtight container for Thursday's Caesar salad. In the skillet, bring the tarragon sauce to a boil. Sprinkle the sauce with chopped tarragon, and serve with the remaining 4 chicken breasts.

WEDNESDAY

Main: Lentil dal

Cooking and reheating time: 10 minutes

Ingredients: the rice, lentil dal, bag of baby spinach, remaining cilantro, salt, and pepper

Cook the rice according to the package directions. Reheat the lentil dal in a saucepan over low heat for 5 minutes. Add the bag of baby spinach, season with salt and pepper, and let cook over high heat for 5 more minutes.

Serve the lentil dal with half the rice and half the cilantro. Place the remaining rice and cilantro in the refrigerator to serve with the monkfish on Friday.

For Thursday, remove the radish-greens spread from the freezer and thaw it in the refrigerator.

THURSDAY

Appetizer: Creamy radish-greens spread

Main: Caesar salad

Reheating time: 10 minutes

Preparation time: 15 minutes

Ingredients: the radish-greens spread, the remaining radish slices, the heads of romaine, the remaining 4 chicken breasts, the croutons, hard-boiled egg, garlic clove, anchovies, wedge of Parmesan, lemon half, sunflower oil, heavy cream, Tabasco sauce, Worcestershire sauce

In a saucepan, reheat the radish-greens spread over low heat for 10 minutes. Distribute the remaining radish slices on top.

Make the Caesar dressing: In the bowl of a food processor, add the peeled hard-boiled egg, half the Parmesan, the garlic, and anchovies. Process until smooth. Add the juice of the lemon half, and process for 2 minutes. Add ⅓ cup (80 mL) of olive oil, the cream, and several drops of Tabasco sauce and Worcestershire sauce. Pulse briefly to combine.

Wash and dry the lettuce leaves. Dress the leaves with some of the Caesar dressing. Cut the chicken breasts into thin strips, and season them with salt and pepper.

In a large bowl, combine the romaine leaves, chicken, and croutons. Using a vegetable peeler, shave off large shavings of the remaining Parmesan. Serve with the remaining dressing on the side.

FRIDAY

Main: Green curry monkfish

Reheating time: 10 minutes

Ingredients: the green curry monkfish, the remaining cilantro, the remaining rice, salt, and pepper

Reheat the monkfish in a saucepan, and reheat the rice according to the method you prefer. Serve the green curry monkfish over the rice. Season with salt and pepper, and sprinkle with the cilantro.

For Friday, remove the green curry monkfish from the freezer and thaw it in the refrigerator.

MENU #3

SHOPPING LIST MENU #3

FRUITS / VEGETABLES

* 1 fennel bulb
* 1 lemon
* 1 lime
* 1 head red leaf lettuce
* 1 bunch carrots
* 1 cup bean sprouts
* 2¼ lb (1 kg) spinach leaves, or 18 oz (500 g) frozen chopped spinach
* 3 tomatoes
* 2 small cucumbers
* 14 oz (400 g) fava beans in their pods, or 7 oz (200 g) shelled and frozen
* 1 bunch green onions
* 1 bunch cilantro
* 1 (2-in./5-cm) knob fresh ginger
* 4 garlic cloves

PANTRY AND STAPLES

* 9 oz (250 g) quick-cooking durum wheat (such as Ebly brand) or other grain
* 7 oz (200 g) conchiglioni (large pasta shells)
* Just over ¾ cup (200 mL) plain tomato sauce
* Dried bread crumbs
* All-purpose flour
* Mustard
* Dried thyme
* Vinegar

* Olive oil
* Sunflower oil
* Soy sauce
* Salt, black pepper

MEAT / FISH

* 4 strips hanger steak
* 4 thin turkey cutlets
* 2 thin slices ham*
* 20 frozen raw, peeled shrimp

  For a pork-free menu, replace the ham with sliced cooked turkey breast.

COLD CASE

* 10 large eggs
* 1 cup (9 oz/250 g) ricotta cheese
* 1 cup (4 oz/113 g) grated Parmesan cheese
* 1 ball (8 oz/227 g) fresh mozzarella cheese
* 1⅓ cups (320 mL) cream
* 1 small log fresh goat cheese (4¼ to 6⅓ oz/ 120 to 180 g), coated with ash

DRY AND CANNED GOODS

* 2 cans albacore tuna (about 11¼ oz/320 g total)
* 8 anchovies
* 1¾ oz (50 g) niçoise olives
* 7 oz (200 g) rice stick noodles (rice vermicelli)
* 1 baguette (purchased the weekend before and frozen, or purchased Thursday)
* Nuoc mam (fish sauce)

MENUS

MONDAY
Appetizer: Fennel marinated in olive oil and lemon

Main: Turkey cordon bleu*

TUESDAY
Marinated hanger steak, puréed baby carrots

WEDNESDAY
Spinach and ricotta–stuffed shells

THURSDAY
Niçoise salad

FRIDAY
Appetizer: Warm goat cheese toasts

Main: Shrimp pad thai

For a pork-free menu, replace the ham with sliced cooked turkey breast.

SET UP

If you have enough work space, set out all the ingredients needed for this cooking session. This includes everything except the lime, bean sprouts, shrimp, 3 eggs, Parmesan, goat cheese, tuna, anchovies, olives, durum wheat, rice stick noodles, and nuoc mam. This allows you to have everything at your fingertips and to not lose time searching for the ingredients in the pantry or refrigerator.

SET OUT THE NECESSARY EQUIPMENT:

* 1 grater (for grating the carrots and ginger)
* 1 large baking dish
* 1 salad spinner (or large bowl and clean kitchen towel)
* 1 mixing bowl
* 1 sauté pan
* 1 small saucepan
* 1 medium saucepan
* 1 large saucepan
* 1 immersion blender
* 1 skimmer
* 1 food processor (or mandoline slicer or knife)
* 3 shallow bowls
* 10 containers: 3 large + 3 medium + 4 small
* 1 freezer bag (if you will be freezing the baguette), plastic wrap, paper towels

EVERYTHING IS NOW READY FOR A COOKING TIME OF 2 HOURS AND 10 MINUTES!

1. Rinse each leaf of the red lettuce under cold water. Gently dry the leaves in the salad spinner (or pat them dry with the kitchen towel), then place them in a large airtight container between two sheets of paper towels; the leaves will keep for up to 1 week in the refrigerator.

2. Remove any rubber bands from around the bunch of cilantro, and immerse the cilantro in cold water to wash it. Gently dry the cilantro in the salad spinner (or pat dry with the towel), set aside 6 sprigs, and place the remaining sprigs in

an airtight container between two sheets of paper towels for up to 1 week.

3. Wash the fresh spinach leaves, spin the leaves dry in the salad spinner (or gently pat dry with the towel), and roughly chop them. Peel and chop the garlic cloves.

4. In the sauté pan, heat 2 tbsp (30 mL) of olive oil until warm. Add ½ tsp of chopped garlic, ½ tsp of salt, and the chopped spinach, a little at a time. Let cook for 15 minutes, uncovered, just until the water released by the spinach has evaporated.

5. Fill the large saucepan with salted water and bring it to a boil. Cook the pasta shells to al dente (still firm to the bite). Drain.

6. Add the cooked spinach to the mixing bowl. Add the ricotta, season with salt and pepper, and process with the immersion blender until roughly blended.

7. Pour the tomato sauce into the large baking dish, and season with salt and pepper. Stuff the pasta shells with the ricotta-spinach mixture using

a small spoon. Snugly arrange the shells in the baking dish.

8. Fill the medium saucepan with salted water and bring it to a boil. Peel all of the carrots. Grate 2 of the carrots and place them in an airtight container. Cut the remaining carrots into rounds, and cook them for 20 minutes in the boiling water.

9. Fill the small saucepan with salted water and bring it to a boil. Shell the beans, and cook them for 2 minutes in the boiling water. Using the skimmer, remove the beans from the saucepan and rinse them under cold water. In the same saucepan of boiling water, cook 4 of the eggs for 10 minutes.

10. Very thinly slice the fennel bulb (using the mandoline, food processor, or knife). Place the slices in a small container and sprinkle them with the juice from the lemon, 3 tbsp (45 mL) of olive oil, ½ tsp of salt, and a little pepper. Stir briefly to combine, and place them in the refrigerator to marinate.

11. Peel the ginger and cut into thirds. Drain the cooked carrots and return them to the saucepan. Using the immersion blender, purée the cooked carrots with the cream, ½ tsp of salt, a little pepper, and one-third of the ginger, and blend until smooth. Transfer to a container.

12. Cut off and discard the root ends of the green onions, and slice them. Place them in a small airtight container.

13. Prepare the marinade for the steak by combining in a container 2 tbsp (30 mL) of soy sauce, 2 tbsp (30 mL) of sunflower oil, the 6 sprigs of cilantro (chopped), 1 tbsp of sliced green onions, one-third of the ginger (grated), and ½ tsp of chopped garlic. Place the hanger steaks into the marinade.

14. Chop the remaining ginger. Place the remaining chopped garlic and chopped ginger into a small airtight container.

15. Wash the cucumbers and cut them into rounds. Slice the tomatoes. Place the sliced cucumbers and tomatoes into a container with the beans (the beans will be protected by their skins).

16. Cut the mozzarella ball into 8 slices. Arrange the three shallow bowls. In the first bowl, add ¼ cup (¾ oz/24 g) of flour. In the second bowl, add 3 eggs, lightly beaten. In the third bowl, add 1 cup (3½ oz/100 g) of dried bread crumbs.

17. Prepare the turkey cordon bleu: Place one turkey cutlet between two rectangular sheets of plastic wrap. Using the bottom of a saucepan, firmly pound on the cutlet to flatten it out. Repeat for each cutlet. Cut the slices of ham or turkey breast in half. Place 1 ham half on top of each turkey cutlet. Place 2 slices of mozzarella on top in the center. Season with salt and pepper. Fold the cutlet over onto itself to close it. Dredge both sides of the cutlet in the flour, shaking off any excess, then dip it into the eggs. Press both sides into the dried bread crumbs to coat. Repeat these steps for each cutlet, then transfer them to a container.

IT'S ALL DONE! LET COOL.

PLACE IN THE REFRIGERATOR:

* The marinated fennel (keeps for 2 days)
* The turkey cordon bleus (keeps for 2 days)
* The marinated steak (keeps for 3 days)
* The carrot purée (keeps for 3 days)
* The stuffed shells, in their baking dish, covered with plastic wrap (keeps for 4 days)
* The hard-boiled eggs (keeps for 5 days)
* The container containing the tomatoes, cucumbers, and beans (keeps for 1 week)
* The sliced green onions (keeps for 1 week)
* The rinsed lettuce (keeps for 1 week)
* The grated carrots (keeps for 1 week)
* The remaining cilantro (keeps for 1 week)
* The small container containing the garlic and chopped ginger (keeps for 1 week)
* The vinaigrette (keeps for 1 week)

PLACE IN THE FREEZER:

* The slices of baguette (if necessary)

18. Make a vinaigrette by combining 2 tbsp (30 g) of mustard, 3 tbsp (45 mL) of vinegar, 1 tsp of salt, and a little pepper. Vigorously whisk the mixture while slowly drizzling in 6 tbsp (90 mL) of olive oil, 1 tbsp (15 mL) at a time, until smooth.

19. If you purchased the baguette over the weekend, slice it, and place the slices into the freezer bag.

EACH NIGHT'S PREP

MONDAY

Appetizer: Fennel marinated in olive oil and lemon

Main: Turkey cordon bleu

Cooking time: 10 minutes

Ingredients: the marinated fennel, olive oil, the turkey cordon bleus, half the lettuce leaves, the vinaigrette

Remove the marinated fennel from the refrigerator at least 15 minutes before serving.

In a skillet, heat 3 tbsp (45 mL) of olive oil until warm. Cook the turkey cordon bleus for 5 minutes on each side over low heat, or until the turkey is cooked through. Serve with the fennel and lettuce leaves dressed with the vinaigrette (reserving some of the vinaigrette for the following days).

TUESDAY

Main: Marinated hanger steak, puréed baby carrots

Reheating time: 10 minutes

Cooking time: 5 minutes

Ingredients: the carrot purée, the sliced green onions, the marinated hanger steak

Reheat the carrot purée in a saucepan or in the microwave. Sprinkle 1 tbsp of the sliced green onions over the top. Cook the hanger steaks in their marinade for 5 minutes over high heat, or until cooked to the desired doneness.

WEDNESDAY

Main: Spinach and ricotta–stuffed shells

Reheating time: 10 minutes

Ingredients: the stuffed shells, the Parmesan

Preheat the oven to 400°F (200°C). Sprinkle the shells with the Parmesan, and bake for 10 minutes, or until browned on top.

THURSDAY

Main: Niçoise salad

Preparation time: 10 minutes

Cooking time: 10 minutes

Ingredients: the durum wheat, the container with the tomatoes, cucumber, and beans, the hard-boiled eggs, the anchovies, the tuna, drained, 4 sprigs of cilantro, the sliced green onions, the olives, the vinaigrette

Cook the durum wheat according to the package directions. Rinse it under cold water to cool. Remove the skins from the beans by pinching them between your fingers. Peel the hard-boiled eggs. Combine all the ingredients in a large bowl, and serve with some of the vinaigrette (reserve a little of the vinaigrette for the next day).

FRIDAY

Appetizer: Warm goat cheese toasts

Main: Shrimp pad thai

Cooking time: 11 minutes

Preparation time: 15 minutes

Ingredients: the baguette, goat cheese log, dried thyme, remaining lettuce leaves, remaining vinaigrette, rice stick noodles, frozen shrimp, sunflower oil, garlic-ginger mixture, grated carrots, soy sauce, nuoc mam, 3 eggs, bean sprouts, remaining green onions, remaining cilantro, lime wedges

Preheat the oven to 400°F (200°C). Toast the baguette slices in the oven for 3 minutes. Cut the goat cheese log into rounds. Place one goat cheese round onto each slice of toasted bread, sprinkle with thyme, and place the bread slices back in the oven for 3 more minutes to melt the cheese. Serve the toasts on top of the lettuce leaves dressed with the vinaigrette.

Place the noodles in very hot water for 5 minutes to rehydrate them.

Rinse and dry the shrimp, then score each down the back using a sharp paring knife. Heat 3 tbsp (45 mL) of sunflower oil in a wok or sauté pan. Add the shrimp, and let them cook for 1 minute over very high heat. Remove the shrimp from the pan and place them in a bowl. Add the garlic-ginger mixture to the wok. Let cook for 1 minute. Add the grated carrots, 4 tbsp (60 mL) of soy sauce, and 4 tbsp (60 mL) of nuoc mam. Add the drained rehydrated noodles and about ¾ cup (180 mL) of water. Let cook for 5 minutes, stirring frequently. Move the noodles to the side of the pan, and break the 3 eggs into the bottom of the pan next to the noodles. Let cook for 2 minutes, then stir to combine the cooked eggs into the noodles. Add the shrimp back to the pan, stir for 30 seconds, then turn off the heat. Add the bean sprouts and green onions, and sprinkle with chopped cilantro. Serve with lime wedges.

MENU #4

SHOPPING LIST   MENU #4

FRUITS / VEGETABLES

* 4 lb (1.8 kg) new potatoes
* 2 cups (9 oz/250 g) small green peas, shelled
* 7 oz (200 g) snow peas
* 3 carrots
* 1 small head cauliflower
* 1 small broccoli crown
* 1 bunch chives
* 1 bunch chervil
* 6 spears green asparagus
* 3½ oz (100 g) baby spinach
* 2 organic lemons
* 3 yellow onions
* 4 garlic cloves

PANTRY AND STAPLES

* 9 oz (250 g) tagliatelle pasta
* 1⅓ cups (9 oz/250 g) white rice
* 2 bay leaves
* Ras el hanout (Moroccan spice blend)
* Ground cumin
* Olive oil
* Wine vinegar
* Salt, black pepper

MEAT / FISH

* 1 veal chop (about 2¼ lb/1 kg)
* 10½ oz (300 g) smoked mackerel fillets
* 14 oz (400 g) boneless, skinless chicken breasts

COLD CASE

* 9 tbsp (4½ oz/125 g) unsalted butter
* 1⅓ cups (320 mL) heavy cream
* 10½ oz (300 g) *fromage frais*, preferably Philadelphia brand (or a good ricotta, mascarpone, or plain yogurt)
* 1 (6-oz/170-g) package feta cheese

DRY AND CANNED GOODS

* 8 slices white sandwich bread
* 1 (15-oz/425-g) can chickpeas
* 1¼ cups (7 oz/200 g) bulgur wheat
* 4 tbsp (1⅔ oz/48 g) capers, drained
* ½ cup (3½ oz/100 g) almonds
* 2 cans crushed tomatoes (about 1¾ lb/800 g)
* 1 oz (30 g) pitted black olives
* 2 chicken bouillon cubes

MENUS

MONDAY
Veal chop with spring vegetables

TUESDAY
Appetizer: Cauliflower in caper vinaigrette

Main: Savory cheesecake

WEDNESDAY
Appetizer: Smoked mackerel rillettes

Main: Chicken puttanesca and rice

THURSDAY
Spiced bulgur with cauliflower, broccoli, and chickpeas

FRIDAY
Smoked mackerel tagliatelle and vegetables

SET UP

If you have enough work space, set out all the ingredients needed for this cooking session. This includes everything except 1 lemon, the cream, tagliatelle, 4 slices of white sandwich bread, chickpeas, bulgur, and rice. This allows you to have everything at your fingertips and to not lose time searching for the ingredients in the pantry or refrigerator.

SET OUT THE NECESSARY EQUIPMENT:

* 1 lidded Dutch oven or stockpot
* 1 sauté pan
* 1 large baking dish
* 1 (8-in./20-cm) removable-bottom tart pan
* 1 food processor
* 1 mixing bowl
* 1 serving bowl
* 1 salad spinner (or a large bowl and clean kitchen towel)
* 1 small grater or zester (for the lemon zest)
* 2 small bowls
* 6 containers: 3 large + 1 medium + 2 small
* 1 small lidded glass jar
* Parchment paper, plastic wrap

EVERYTHING IS NOW READY FOR A COOKING TIME OF 1 HOUR AND 55 MINUTES!

1. Preheat the oven to 350°F (180°C). Place 4 slices of the sandwich bread and the almonds in the large baking dish. Bake for 10 minutes, or until golden. Remove the bread and almonds, and set them aside. Leave the oven on.

2. Peel the onions and garlic cloves. Thinly slice them, and place them in two separate bowls.

3. In the Dutch oven, heat 3 tbsp (45 mL) of olive oil until warm. Season the veal chop on both sides with salt and pepper, and cook it over high heat until browned, about 5 minutes on each side.

4. Remove the veal chop from the pot, and add one-third of the sliced onions and garlic to the pan

along with 1 tsp of salt. Cook for 5 minutes over low heat, or until slightly softened.

5. Meanwhile, peel the potatoes and carrots. Cut the carrots into thick rounds and cut the potatoes in half. Place the potatoes and carrots in the pot. Add just over ¾ cup (200 mL) of water, 1 chicken bouillon cube, and the bay leaves. Place the veal chop back in the pot, cover, and let cook gently over low heat for 20 minutes.

6. In the large baking dish, place the crushed tomatoes, black olives, half the remaining garlic and onions, and 2 tbsp (¾ oz/24g) of the capers. Drizzle everything with 3 tbsp (45 mL) of olive oil, season with salt and pepper, and stir briefly to coat. Bake for 35 minutes.

7. In the food processor, place the toasted bread and half the toasted almonds. Process until the mixture is reduced to fine crumbs. Melt the butter. Add three-fourths of the melted butter to the food processor and process briefly to combine. Set the remaining butter aside.

8. Cut out a circle of parchment paper the diameter of the bottom of the tart pan. Place the parchment circle on the bottom of the pan, and cover it with the toasted bread and almond mixture. Using the bottom of a drinking glass, gently press the mixture down into the pan, allowing the mixture to rise up the sides of the pan. Place the pan in the refrigerator.

9. Wash the bowl of the food processor to prepare the rillettes. In the food processor, place half (5¼ oz/150 g) of the mackerel fillets (skinned), 3½ oz (100 g) of the *fromage frais*, the remaining melted butter, and the zest of 1 lemon and two-thirds of its juice. Process briefly to combine.

10. Wash the chives and chervil and gently dry them in the salad spinner, or pat them dry using the clean kitchen towel. Chop one-third of the chives and sprinkle them over the mackerel mixture (rillettes). Stir to combine, and place the mixture in the serving bowl.

11. To the Dutch oven, add the snow peas and half the shelled green peas, and let cook for 15 more minutes, or until the veal is cooked through.

12. Slice the chicken breasts, add the slices to the large baking dish, and stir to combine. Continue baking for 10 more minutes, or until the chicken is cooked through.

13. Wash the food processor to prepare the savory cheesecake. In the food processor, place the remaining *fromage frais*, half the feta, and the remaining juice of the lemon. Process until well combined, then transfer the mixture to the mixing bowl. Chop half the remaining chives and stir them into the mixture using a spatula. Remove the tart pan from the refrigerator, and spread the cream cheese mixture into the bottom of the pan.

14. Wash the baby spinach and dry the leaves in the salad spinner (or fill a large bowl with water and wash the leaves, then gently pat them dry with the kitchen towel). Top the baking dish with half

the baby spinach, and continue baking for 2 more minutes, or until the leaves are wilted.

15. In the sauté pan, heat 2 tbsp (30 mL) of olive oil until warm. Add the remaining chopped onions, 1 tbsp (¼ oz/7 g) of the ras el hanout, and ½ tsp of salt. Cook for 5 minutes over low heat. Cut the broccoli crown and cauliflower into florets, and add them to the sauté pan with the remaining bouillon cube. Add just enough water to cover the vegetables, and cook, covered, for 15 minutes.

16. Prepare the caper vinaigrette: Combine 4 tbsp (60 mL) of olive oil, 2 tbsp (30 mL) of wine vinegar, ½ tsp of cumin, and the remaining capers. Season with salt and pepper.

17. Using a knife, roughly chop the remaining toasted almonds. Set them aside in the small glass jar.

18. Peel the asparagus, cut off and discard the tough stem end, cut the asparagus crosswise in half, then cut the sections lengthwise in half.

PLACE IN THE FREEZER:

* The chicken puttanesca, preferably in its baking dish, wrapped in plastic wrap

PANTRY:

* The toasted almonds

IT'S ALL DONE! LET COOL.

PLACE IN THE REFRIGERATOR:

* The raw green vegetables: the remaining peas, the baby spinach, and the peeled asparagus spears
* The veal chop, in its pot
* Half the cooked cauliflower, without the cooking water (keeps for 4 days)
* The cooked broccoli and cauliflower in their cooking water (keeps for 4 days)
* The smoked mackerel rillettes (keeps for 5 days)
* The savory cheesecake (keeps for 3 days)
* The remaining chives and chervil (keeps for 1 week)
* The caper vinaigrette (keeps for 1 week)
* The remaining smoked mackerel, loosely wrapped
* The remaining feta, loosely wrapped

EACH NIGHT'S PREP

MONDAY

Main: Veal chop with spring vegetables

Reheating time: 15 minutes

Ingredients: the pot with the veal chop and vegetables, salt, and pepper

Reheat the veal chop and vegetables for 15 minutes over medium heat. Season with salt and pepper, and serve.

TUESDAY

Appetizer: Cauliflower in caper vinaigrette

Main: Savory cheesecake

Cooking time: 5 minutes

Preparation time: 3 minutes

Ingredients: the caper vinaigrette, the cooked cauliflower, 4 sprigs of chives, the container with the raw green vegetables, 4 sprigs of chervil, the savory cheesecake

Pour the vinaigrette over the cauliflower, top with chopped chives, and stir to combine. Serve.

Bring a saucepan of salted water to a boil. Cook half the asparagus pieces and half the green peas in the boiling water for 5 minutes; they should remain somewhat firm. Chop the chervil and sprinkle it over the cheesecake for garnish. Serve with the cooked peas and asparagus and some of the baby spinach. Place the remaining raw vegetables in the refrigerator to serve on Friday.

For Wednesday, remove the chicken puttanesca from the freezer and thaw it in the refrigerator.

WEDNESDAY

Appetizer: Smoked mackerel rillettes

Main: Chicken puttanesca and rice

Reheating time: 10 minutes

Cooking time: 15 minutes

Preparation time: 5 minutes

Ingredients: the 4 remaining slices of sandwich bread, the smoked mackerel rillettes, 4 sprigs of chervil, the chicken puttanesca, the rice

Toast the bread in a toaster. Cut the toasts into quarters. Spread the smoked mackerel rillettes on top of the toast pieces, sprinkle them with chopped chervil, and serve.

Preheat the oven to 350°F (180°C). Reheat the chicken puttanesca for 10 minutes. Cook the rice according to the package directions, and serve on the side with the chicken puttanesca.

THURSDAY

Main: Spiced bulgur with cauliflower, broccoli, and chickpeas

Cooking time: 10 minutes

Reheating time: 5 minutes

Preparation time: 3 minutes

Ingredients: the bulgur, the can of chickpeas, the cooked broccoli and cauliflower with their liquid, the toasted almonds, half the remaining chives and chervil.

Cook the bulgur according to the package directions (in general about 10 minutes in boiling salted water). Drain and rinse the chickpeas. Add the chickpeas to the container with the broccoli and cauliflower. Reheat for 5 minutes in the microwave. Spoon the broccoli, cauliflower, and chickpeas over the bulgur. Sprinkle with the toasted almonds. Chop the herbs and sprinkle them over the top.

FRIDAY

Main: Smoked mackerel tagliatelle and vegetables

Cooking time: 15 minutes

Preparation time: 10 minutes

Ingredients: the tagliatelle, the remaining raw green vegetables, the remaining smoked mackerel, 1 lemon, the remaining feta, the remaining fresh herbs, the cream, salt and pepper

Bring a large saucepan of salted water to a boil. Cook the tagliatelle in boiling water with the asparagus and green peas. Two minutes before the end of the cooking time, add the baby spinach.

Meanwhile, slice the smoked mackerel. Zest and juice the lemon. Dice the feta into small cubes. Chop the fresh herbs. Drain the pasta and vegetables and add them to a large bowl. Add the cream, the lemon zest and juice, the mackerel slices, the diced feta, and the chopped fresh herbs to the bowl. Season with salt and pepper, stir to combine, and serve.

SUMMER

MENU #1

SHOPPING LIST — MENU #1

FRUITS / VEGETABLES

* 4 large, or 8 medium, round tomatoes, for stuffing
* 4 on-the-vine tomatoes
* 6 zucchini
* 1 eggplant
* 5 red bell peppers
* 3 large potatoes
* 1 cucumber
* 1 lemon
* 1 bunch cilantro
* 1 bunch basil
* 6 garlic cloves
* 4 yellow onions

PANTRY AND STAPLES

* 14 oz (400 g) plain tomato sauce
* 16 oz (454 g) short pasta (such as penne)
* 1⅓ cups (9 oz/250 g) white rice
* 1 cup (5¼ oz/150 g) white quinoa
* Herbes de Provence
* Wine vinegar
* Olive oil
* Salt, black pepper

MEAT / FISH

* 4 large chicken thighs
* 14 oz (400 g) ground veal (or beef)
* 8 thin slices ham* (such as di Parma; pressed; with herbs; prosciutto; etc.)

  For a pork-free menu, replace the prosciutto with sliced cooked turkey breast.

COLD CASE

* Just over ¾ cup (6 oz/170 g) crème fraiche or plain yogurt
* 1 small round goat cheese (about 2 oz/60 g)
* 1 (6-oz/170-g) package feta cheese
* 1 (5¼-oz/150-g) bag shredded mozzarella cheese
* 2 balls pizza dough (about 14 oz/400 g each)
* 1 prepared puff pastry sheet (about 8 oz/227 g)

DRY AND CANNED GOODS

* 5¼ oz (150 g) pitted black olives

MENUS

MONDAY
Appetizer: Quinoa tabbouleh
Main: Chicken thighs and ratatouille

TUESDAY
Prosciutto di Parma* and vegetable pizza

WEDNESDAY
Zucchini, olive, and chicken pasta

THURSDAY
Appetizer: Goat cheese and ratatouille turnovers
Main: Stuffed tomatoes and rice

FRIDAY
Family-size vegetable pasta salad

For a pork-free menu, replace the prosciutto with sliced cooked turkey breast.

SET UP

If you have enough work space, set out all the ingredients needed for this cooking session. This includes everything except the ham, puff pastry (keep refrigerated until right before using), pizza dough, crème fraîche, feta, mozzarella, olives, rice, tomato sauce, and pasta. This allows you to have everything at your fingertips and to not lose time searching for the ingredients in the pantry or refrigerator.

SET OUT THE NECESSARY EQUIPMENT:

* 1 baking sheet
* 1 large saucepan
* 1 skillet
* 1 lidded Dutch oven or stockpot
* 2 small bowls
* 1 gratin baking dish (or shallow baking dish)
* 1 salad spinner (or clean kitchen towel)
* 1 fine-mesh strainer
* 1 drinking glass 3 to 4 in. (8 to 10 cm) in diameter
* 10 containers: 3 small + 5 medium + 2 large
* Paper towels, parchment paper

EVERYTHING IS NOW READY FOR A COOKING TIME OF 1 HOUR AND 30 MINUTES!

1. Preheat the oven to 400°F (200°C).

2. Peel all of the onions and garlic cloves and cut them into small dice. Put the onions in one small bowl and the garlic in the other.

3. Arrange the chicken thighs on the baking sheet lined with parchment paper. Sprinkle the thighs generously with the herbes de Provence. Season with salt. Bake for 40 minutes, or until cooked through.

4. Prepare the ratatouille: In the Dutch oven, heat 2 tbsp (30 mL) of olive oil until warm. Add half the diced onions and garlic, then add 1 tbsp of salt. Cook gently until slightly softened.

5. Meanwhile, wash the bell peppers, cut them in half, remove and discard the seeds and white membrane, and cut into small dice. Add 3 of the diced bell peppers to the pot. Place the remaining bell peppers in an airtight container, and refrigerate.

6. Wash the zucchini. Cut off and discard the ends, and cut the zucchini into small dice. Add 3 of the diced zucchini to the pot. Place the remaining diced zucchini in an airtight container, and refrigerate.

7. Wash the tomatoes for stuffing. Cut off the tops and set them aside. Using a spoon, scoop out the flesh of the tomatoes and add it to the pot. Season inside the tomatoes with salt, and place them upside down on a plate lined with a paper towel to drain any excess liquid.

8. Wash the eggplant, cut it into small dice, and add it to the pot.

9. Peel the potatoes, cut them into small dice, and add them to the pot. Cover the pot, and let simmer for 35 minutes, stirring occasionally.

10. Place the basil and cilantro in the salad spinner, then wash and gently dry them (or rinse under cool water and dry with the clean kitchen towel). Place all of the basil and half the cilantro in an airtight container between two sheets of paper towels. Place the container in the refrigerator for up to 1 week.

11. Prepare the stuffing for the tomatoes: In the skillet, heat 1 tbsp (15 mL) of olive oil until warm. Add the remaining diced onions, half the remaining garlic, and 1 tsp of salt. Cook for 5 minutes, or until slightly softened. Meanwhile, chop the remaining cilantro. Add the ground veal and the cilantro to the skillet. Let cook for 10 minutes, stirring frequently.

12. Bring 6 cups (1.5 L) of salted water to a boil in the large saucepan. Thoroughly rinse the quinoa.

13. Peel the cucumber and cut it into small dice. Wash the on-the-vine tomatoes, and cut them into small dice. Store the cucumbers and tomatoes separately in airtight containers (to serve with the salads).

14. Cook the quinoa in the boiling water for 15 minutes, or until tender.

15. Fill the tomatoes with the stuffing mixture, and place them in the baking dish. Replace the tops, and bake for 30 minutes, or until somewhat shriveled and the meat is cooked through. Remove the chicken thighs from the oven at the same time, and let cool.

16. Spoon 6 tbsp of the ratatouille into the fine-mesh strainer, and press down with the back of a spoon to release as much liquid as possible; set aside.

17. Prepare the lemon sauce for the tabbouleh: Combine the juice from the lemon with 2 tbsp (30 mL) of olive oil, ½ tsp of salt, and a little pepper.

18. Unroll the puff pastry sheet. Cut out nine 4-in. (10-cm) circles using the rim of the drinking glass. Cut the goat cheese into small dice. Spoon some of the goat cheese into the center of each dough circle. Top the goat cheese with 2 tsp of the drained ratatouille, and sprinkle the top with herbes de Provence. Fold one side of each dough circle over the filling to form a turnover. Seal the edges by gently pressing them with the tines of a fork. Bake for 20 minutes, or until golden and flaky.

19. Drain the quinoa and rinse it under cold water. Place it in an airtight container.

20. Shred the flesh of 2 of the chicken thighs, and set it aside in an airtight container.

IT'S ALL DONE! LET COOL.

PLACE IN THE REFRIGERATOR:

* The cooked quinoa (keeps for 2 days)
* The lemon sauce for the quinoa tabbouleh (keeps for 3 days)

* The containers of raw vegetables: bell peppers, zucchini, tomatoes, and cucumbers (keeps for 1 week)

* The ratatouille, in its pot (keeps for 3 days)

* The 2 whole chicken thighs, in an airtight container (keeps for 2 days)

* The basil and cilantro, in an airtight container (keeps for 1 week)

* The remaining garlic, in a small airtight container (keeps for 1 week)

PLACE IN THE FREEZER:

* The goat cheese and ratatouille turnovers
* The stuffed tomatoes
* The shredded chicken meat

MENU #1

EACH NIGHT'S PREP

MONDAY

Appetizer: Quinoa tabbouleh

Main: Chicken thighs and ratatouille

Reheating time: 15 minutes

Preparation time: 2 minutes

Ingredients: the pot of ratatouille, the whole chicken thighs, half the cilantro, the cooked quinoa, the containers of diced tomatoes, cucumber, and bell peppers, the lemon sauce

Reheat the ratatouille in its pot, and reheat the chicken thighs either in the oven preheated to 350°F (180°C) or in the pot with the ratatouille.

Chop the cilantro. In a large bowl, combine the quinoa, cilantro, half the containers of diced tomatoes and cucumber, and one-fourth of the diced bell peppers. Pour the lemon sauce over the top, and stir to combine.

TUESDAY

Main: Prosciutto di Parma and vegetable pizza

Cooking time: 10 minutes

Preparation time: 10 minutes

Ingredients: the 2 balls of pizza dough, the tomato sauce, the container of zucchini and bell peppers, a little of the herbes de Provence, a few black olives (optional), the shredded mozzarella, the ham slices (or turkey), and 2 sprigs of basil

Preheat the oven to 400°F (200°C). Meanwhile, roll out the pizza dough and cover each dough circle with some of the tomato sauce, leaving a ¾-in. (2-cm) border. Divide half the zucchini and half the bell peppers and distribute them on top (place the remaining in the refrigerator). Sprinkle with herbes de Provence and distribute several black olives, if using, on top. Top with the shredded mozzarella. Bake for 10 minutes, then place 4 slices of the ham and several basil leaves on top.

For Wednesday, remove the shredded chicken meat from the freezer and thaw it in the refrigerator.

WEDNESDAY

Main: Zucchini, olive, and chicken pasta

Cooking and reheating time: 15 minutes

Preparation time: 2 minutes

Ingredients: the package of pasta, olive oil, the remaining garlic, the container of zucchini, the thawed shredded chicken meat, the crème fraîche, 1 handful of black olives, half the basil, salt, and pepper

Cook the pasta in a large saucepan filled with salted water. Meanwhile, heat 1 tbsp (15 mL) of olive oil in a sauté pan until warm. Add the garlic and all of the zucchini. Let cook for 10 minutes, or until softened. Drain the pasta. Set aside half the pasta in an airtight container (for the pasta salad on Friday). To the sauté pan, add the chicken meat, crème fraîche, olives, and pasta. Season with salt and pepper. Cook for 2 minutes. Sprinkle with basil.

For Thursday, remove the goat cheese and ratatouille turnovers and the stuffed tomatoes from the freezer and thaw them in the refrigerator.

THURSDAY

Appetizer: Goat cheese and ratatouille turnovers

Main: Stuffed tomatoes and rice

Reheating time: 15 minutes

Cooking time: 10 minutes

Ingredients: The goat cheese and ratatouille turnovers, the stuffed tomatoes, the rice

Reheat the turnovers and the stuffed tomatoes in the oven preheated to 325°F (160°C). Cook the rice according to the package directions.

FRIDAY

Main: Family-size vegetable pasta salad

Preparation time: 5 minutes

Ingredients: the feta, the remaining cilantro and basil, the cooked pasta, the container of cucumber and bell peppers, the remaining black olives, olive oil, wine vinegar, salt and pepper

Dice the feta. Chop the cilantro and basil. Place all the ingredients in a large bowl. Drizzle with 2 tbsp (30 mL) of olive oil and 1 tbsp (15 mL) of vinegar.

Season with salt and pepper, and toss to combine.

MENU #2

FRUITS / VEGETABLES

* 4 large eggplants
* 4 zucchini
* 3⅓ lb (1.5 kg) large Charlotte potatoes (or similar waxy salad potato)
* 18 oz (500 g) string beans (fresh or frozen)
* 9 oz (250 g) white button mushrooms
* 4 cups (18 oz/500 g) shelled peas (fresh or frozen)
* 1 cucumber
* 1 small container assorted cherry tomatoes (about 6 oz/170 g)
* 1 bunch green onions
* 1 small bag mesclun (about 5 oz/140 g)
* 1 bunch mint
* 1 bunch dill
* 1 lemon
* 3 garlic cloves
* 2 red onions

PANTRY AND STAPLES

* 9 oz (250 g) plain tomato sauce
* 2 cups (14 oz/400 g) green lentils
* 1⅓ cups (9 oz/250 g) white or light brown rice
* 1½ cups (6⅓ oz/180 g) dried bread crumbs
* Whole nutmeg
* Wine vinegar
* Olive oil
* Ground cinnamon
* Salt, black pepper

MEAT / FISH

* 2¼ lb (1 kg) ground beef
* 4 fresh skinless salmon fillets
* 2 fresh cod loins (10½ oz/300 g total)

COLD CASE

* 1½ tbsp (1 oz/25 g) unsalted butter
* 1⅓ cups (320 mL) heavy cream
* 1 (6-oz/170-g) package feta cheese
* 1 cup (9 oz/250 g) ricotta cheese
* ½ cup (2 oz/60 g) grated Parmesan cheese
* 4 large eggs

DRY AND CANNED GOODS

* 1 can crushed tomatoes (about 14 oz/400 g)

MENUS

MONDAY

Family-size potato, salmon, mesclun, onion, and cucumber salad

TUESDAY

Appetizer: Greek lentil salad

Main: Stuffed zucchini

WEDNESDAY

Moussaka

THURSDAY

Fish blanquette with dill and rice

FRIDAY

Appetizer: Pea, feta, and mint soup

Main: Lentil meatballs in tomato sauce with string beans

SET UP

If you have enough work space, set out all the ingredients needed for this cooking session. This includes everything except the string beans, cherry tomatoes, mesclun, lemon, tomato sauce, and rice. This allows you to have everything at your fingertips and to not lose time searching for the ingredients in the pantry or refrigerator.

SET OUT THE NECESSARY EQUIPMENT:

* 2 baking sheets
* 2 small bowls
* 1 steam cooker or lidded stockpot with a steam basket
* 1 large baking dish
* 1 sauté pan
* 1 large saucepan
* 1 small skillet
* 1 food processor
* 1 immersion blender

* 1 fine-mesh strainer
* 1 salad spinner (or large bowl and clean kitchen towel)
* 1 (6-cup/1.5-L-capacity) glass jar (for storing the pea soup)
* 6 containers: 3 large + 3 medium
* Paper towels, parchment paper, plastic wrap

EVERYTHING IS NOW READY FOR A COOKING TIME OF 2 HOURS!

1. Preheat the oven to 400°F (200°C). Wash the eggplants, and cut them lengthwise into strips measuring ¾-in. (2-cm) thick. Place the strips on the two baking sheets lined with parchment paper. Brush them with a little olive oil and season with salt. Bake for 30 minutes, or until somewhat shriveled and lightly browned.

2. Wash the zucchini. Cut them lengthwise in half. Using a small spoon, scoop out the flesh from

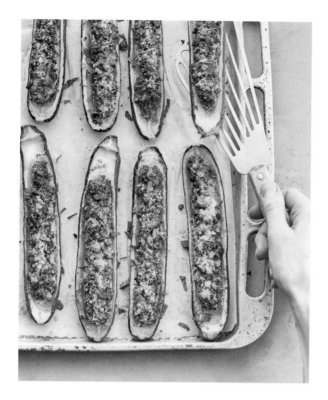

the centers. Place the hollowed halves in the oven next to the eggplants, and bake for 10 minutes.

3. Soak the mint and dill in water for 5 minutes, then spin them dry in the salad spinner (or dry with the kitchen towel). Place half the mint and dill in an airtight container between two sheets of paper towels. Refrigerate for up to 1 week. Chop the remaining mint and dill and place each separately in the small bowls.

4. Peel the potatoes. Steam them for about 20 minutes, or until tender when pierced with a fork. Peel the red onions and cut them in half. Cut 3 onion halves into small dice, and the remaining half into thin slices.

5. Fill the large saucepan with salted water and bring it to a boil. Meanwhile, peel and finely chop the garlic cloves. Set them aside. Rinse the lentils in the fine-mesh strainer. Cook the lentils in the saucepan of boiling water according to the package directions. Do not salt them until the end of the cooking time. Drain, and let cool.

6. In the sauté pan, heat 2 tbsp (30 mL) of olive oil until warm. Add two-thirds of the diced red onions and half the chopped garlic. Season with salt and pepper, and let cook for 5 minutes, or until slightly softened.

7. Meanwhile, peel the cucumber and cut it into small dice. Set it aside in an airtight container.

8. To the sauté pan, add two-thirds of the ground beef, and let cook 10 minutes. Using the remaining ground beef, prepare the stuffing for the zucchini: Combine the meat with 1 egg, 4 tbsp (1 oz/30 g) of dried bread crumbs, half the remaining chopped garlic and red onions, and 2 tbsp of chopped mint. Season with salt and pepper.

9. Fill the precooked zucchini with the stuffing mixture. Sprinkle the top with half the grated Parmesan, and bake for 15 minutes, or until the meat is cooked through.

10. To the sauté pan, add the crushed tomatoes, ¼ tsp of cinnamon, and a little salt. Let cook gently for 20 minutes.

11. Cut one-fourth of the steamed potatoes into rounds, and cut the remaining into large dice.

12. Prepare the cream for the moussaka: Combine half the ricotta cheese with 2 eggs, 1¾ oz (50 g) of feta (crumbled), and 2 tbsp of the remaining grated Parmesan.

13. In the baking dish, place one-third of the eggplant strips and all of the potato slices in a single layer. Top with half the tomato and ground beef mixture, then another third of the eggplant slices, then the remaining meat mixture. Layer the remaining eggplant slices on top, and pour the cream for the moussaka over the top. Bake for 25 minutes, or until golden on top.

14. Rinse the green onions, cut off and discard the root ends, strip off the first layer of skin, then chop the onions. Briefly wash the mushrooms, cut off and discard the stems, then cut the tops in half.

15. Rinse and wipe out the sauté pan. In the pan, melt the butter. Add half the chopped green onions, the mushrooms, and ½ tsp of salt. Cook gently for 2 minutes. Add the chopped dill, heavy cream, 1 handful of the peas, and a scant ¼ cup (50 mL) of water to the sauté pan. Cook over gentle heat for 5 minutes.

16. Meanwhile, cut the cod and salmon into large dice. Add the fish to the sauté pan, and cook with the cream and vegetables for 5 more minutes.

17. Prepare the lentil meatballs: In the food processor, place half the cooked lentils, the remaining ricotta cheese, 1 egg, the remaining garlic and diced red onions, 1 cup (4½ oz/125 g) of the dried bread crumbs, and 1 tbsp of the chopped mint. Season with salt and pepper. Process to combine. Using your hands, form the mixture into meatballs. Roll them in a little of the remaining dried bread crumbs. In the skillet, heat 1 tbsp (15 mL) of olive oil until warm. Cook the meatballs for 10 minutes, browning them on all sides.

PLACE IN THE REFRIGERATOR:

* The diced cucumbers (keeps for 1 week)
* The container with the remaining cooked lentils and the red onion slices
* The container with the diced potatoes, salmon, and green onions (keeps for 2 days)
* The stuffed zucchini, if you serve them within 2 days of preparing them
* The mint and fresh dill in an airtight container (keeps for 1 week)

PLACE IN THE FREEZER:

* The stuffed zucchini, if you will serve them more than 2 days after preparing them
* The soup
* The lentil meatballs
* The moussaka, in its baking dish, covered with plastic wrap
* The fish blanquette

18. Meanwhile, bring 4 cups (1 L) of salted water to a simmer. Place the remaining cooked lentils in an airtight container with the red onion slices.

19. Add the remaining peas and half the remaining chopped green onions to the simmering water. Let cook for 15 minutes, then add 1 handful of the diced potatoes, the remaining chopped mint, and 1½ oz (40 g) of the feta. Blend thoroughly using the immersion blender, then strain. Transfer the mixture to the glass jar, leaving a little room at the top.

20. From the sauté pan with the fish blanquette, remove half the diced fish. Place it in a large container with the remaining diced potatoes and the remaining chopped green onions.

EACH NIGHT'S PREP

MONDAY

Main: Family-size potato, salmon, mesclun, onion, and cucumber salad

Preparation time: 5 minutes

Ingredients: the lemon, olive oil, the container with the diced potatoes, salmon, and onions, the bag of mesclun, half the diced cucumber, half the remaining dill, salt, and pepper

Prepare the sauce: In a large bowl, vigorously whisk together the juice of the lemon with 3 tbsp (45 mL) of olive oil, ½ tsp of salt, and 1 pinch of pepper. Add the remaining ingredients, and toss to coat.

For Tuesday, if you have frozen the stuffed zucchini, remove them from the freezer and thaw them in the refrigerator.

TUESDAY

Appetizer: Greek lentil salad

Main: Stuffed zucchini

Reheating time: 15 minutes

Preparation time: 10 minutes

Ingredients: the stuffed zucchini, olive oil, vinegar, the cherry tomatoes, the cooked lentils with the red onion slices, the remaining cucumber, the remaining feta, the mint, salt, and pepper

Reheat the stuffed zucchini in the oven preheated to 325°F (160°C). In a large bowl, vigorously whisk together 3 tbsp (45 mL) of olive oil with 1 tbsp (15 mL) of vinegar, 1 tsp of salt, and 1 pinch of pepper. Cut the cherry tomatoes in half. Dice three-fourths of the remaining feta, and place the package back in the refrigerator. Chop three-fourths of the mint, and place the remaining in the refrigerator. In a large bowl, combine the cherry tomatoes, lentils, red onion slices, diced cucumber, diced feta, and half the chopped mint.

Sprinkle a little of the mint over the top of the warm stuffed zucchini.

For Wednesday, remove the moussaka from the freezer and thaw it in the refrigerator.

WEDNESDAY

Main: Moussaka

Reheating time: 15 minutes

Ingredients: the moussaka

Reheat the moussaka in the oven preheated to 325°F (160°C), and serve.

For Thursday, remove the fish blanquette from the freezer, and thaw it in the refrigerator.

THURSDAY

Main: Fish blanquette with dill and rice

Reheating time: 10 minutes

Cooking time: 15 minutes

Preparation time: 3 minutes

Ingredients: the thawed fish blanquette, the rice, the remaining dill

Reheat the fish blanquette in a saucepan over very low heat for 10 minutes. Meanwhile, cook the rice according to the package directions. Sprinkle with dill, and serve.

For Friday, remove the pea soup and the meatballs from the freezer and thaw them in the refrigerator.

FRIDAY

Appetizer: Pea, feta, and mint soup

Main: Lentil meatballs in tomato sauce with string beans

Reheating time: 10 minutes

Cooking time: 15 minutes

Preparation time: 10 minutes

Ingredients: the soup, the remaining feta, the remaining mint, the string beans, the tomato sauce, the meatballs, salt, and pepper

In a saucepan, reheat the soup. Serve it with the remaining feta crumbled over the top, a little pepper, and chopped mint. Bring 6 cups (1.5 L) of salted water to a boil, and cook the string beans. In a saucepan, place the tomato sauce, and add ½ tsp of salt and 1 pinch of pepper. Let cook for 5 minutes, until reduced. Add the meatballs, and heat through, about 5 more minutes.

MENU #3

SHOPPING LIST   MENU #3

FRUITS / VEGETABLES

* 3 eggplants
* 1¾ lb (800 g) large Charlotte potatoes (or similar waxy salad potato)
* 2 red bell peppers
* 2 yellow bell peppers
* 2 green bell peppers
* 4 zucchini
* 1 small container cherry tomatoes (about 6 oz/170 g)
* 1 small bag arugula (about 5 oz/140 g)
* 1 bunch cilantro
* 1 bunch basil
* 1 small lemon
* 6 garlic cloves
* 4 yellow onions
* 1 (1-in./3-cm) knob fresh ginger

PANTRY AND STAPLES

* 9 oz (250 g) spaghetti noodles
* 9 oz (250 g) quick-cooking durum wheat (such as Ebly brand) or other grain

* 1⅓ cups (9 oz/250 g) couscous
* Soy sauce
* Honey
* Ground cumin
* Ground coriander seeds
* Whole nutmeg
* Olive oil
* Salt, black pepper

MEAT / FISH

* 8 merguez sausages
* 8 slices bresaola (a thin-sliced, air-dried salted beef)
* 4 boneless, skinless chicken breasts

COLD CASE

* 6 large eggs
* 1 ball (8 oz/227 g) fresh mozzarella cheese
* 1 cup (240 mL) heavy cream

DRY AND CANNED GOODS

* 1 large loaf rustic bread
* Tahini (ground sesame seed paste; optional)

MENUS

MONDAY

Marinated chicken kebabs, durum wheat with roasted vegetables

TUESDAY

Merguez sausage, couscous

WEDNESDAY

Appetizer: Eggplant caviar

Main: Spanish omelet

THURSDAY

Summer bruschetta

FRIDAY

Appetizer: Bell peppers marinated in garlic and olive oil

Main: Tunisian spaghetti

SET UP

If you have enough work space, set out all the ingredients needed for this cooking session. This includes everything except the arugula, bresaola, mozzarella, spaghetti noodles, durum wheat, and couscous. This allows you to have everything at your fingertips and to not lose time searching for the ingredients in the pantry or refrigerator.

SET OUT THE NECESSARY EQUIPMENT:

* 2 large baking sheets
* 1 (8-in./20-cm) round cake pan
* 1 food processor
* 2 large serving bowls
* 1 salad spinner (or large bowl and clean kitchen towel)
* 1 skillet
* 4 kebab skewers (optional)
* 1 small grater or zester (for the nutmeg)
* 4 containers: 2 large + 2 medium
* 2 freezer bags
* Paper towels, parchment paper, plastic wrap

EVERYTHING IS NOW READY FOR A COOKING TIME OF 1 HOUR AND 45 MINUTES!

1. Preheat the oven broiler. Cut the red, yellow, and green bell peppers in half, and remove and discard the seeds and white membranes. On a baking sheet lined with parchment paper, place 2 of the whole eggplants and the bell pepper halves, skin side up. Bake directly under the broiler for 30 minutes, or until the skins are nicely browned.

2. Wash and dry the zucchini, the remaining eggplant, and the cherry tomatoes. Peel the potatoes. Peel the onions and garlic cloves.

3. Dice the zucchini and the eggplant. Thinly slice the onions, and roughly chop the garlic. Cut the potatoes into thin rounds.

4. Place the basil and cilantro in the salad spinner (or a large bowl) filled with water. Soak the

cilantro for 5 minutes. Drain the water, then gently spin the herbs dry (or dry with the kitchen towel). Place the basil and cilantro in an airtight container between two sheets of paper towels. Refrigerate for up to 1 week.

5. Remove the bell peppers and eggplants from the oven. Set them aside on a plate to cool.

6. Preheat the oven to 400°F (200°C). Line the two baking sheets with parchment paper. On one of the lined baking sheets, arrange all of the potato rounds and one-fourth of the following ingredients: the zucchini, cherry tomatoes, onions, and garlic. On the other baking sheet, place the remaining zucchini, cherry tomatoes, onions, and half the chopped garlic. Drizzle 2 tbsp (30 mL) of olive oil over the vegetables on each baking sheet, season with salt and pepper, and stir briefly to coat. Bake for 30 minutes, or until the vegetables are lightly browned.

7. Make the marinade for the chicken: Peel and grate the ginger. In a large container, combine 4 tbsp (60 mL) of soy sauce, 1 tbsp (15 mL) of olive oil, 1 tbsp (20 g) of honey, the freshly grated ginger, and one-third of the remaining garlic. Dice the chicken into equal-size pieces. Place the diced chicken in the marinade, stir to combine, then transfer it to an airtight container.

8. Prepare the eggplant caviar: Scoop out the flesh of the whole eggplants. Place the flesh in the food processor with half the remaining garlic, the juice of the lemon, 1 tbsp (15 g) of tahini (if using), ½ tsp of cumin, and 1 tbsp (15 mL) of olive oil. Process until smooth. Transfer the mixture to a serving dish, and cover it with plastic wrap.

9. Peel the skins from all the bell peppers. Cut the flesh into strips. Place the strips of green bell peppers aside (they will be used for the Tunisian spaghetti). Place half the red and yellow bell pepper strips in an attractive bowl. Add 3 tbsp (45 mL) of olive oil, the remaining chopped garlic, and 1 tsp of salt. Stir to combine, cover with plastic wrap, and refrigerate. Dice the remaining strips of red and yellow bell peppers.

10. In the large bowl, beat the eggs with a whisk. Add the cream. Season with salt and pepper, then add 1 pinch of freshly grated nutmeg.

11. Lower the oven temperature to 350°F (180°C). Grease the bottom and sides of the cake pan. Cut out a circle of parchment paper the diameter of the bottom of the pan and place it in the pan. Distribute the roasted vegetables from the first sheet pan in step six in the cake pan, then scrape the egg mixture over the vegetables. Bake for 30 minutes, or until golden on top.

12. Cut 4 of the sausages into ⅓-in. (1-cm)-long pieces. Leave the 4 remaining sausages whole. Heat the skillet without any added fat, and cook the sausage pieces and the whole sausages until cooked through. Remove the whole sausages from the skillet and set them aside. To the skillet, add the strips of green bell peppers. Let cook just until all of the liquid has evaporated. Transfer the cooked mixture from the skillet to an airtight container.

13. To the same container, add nearly all of the cherry tomatoes and several of the roasted vegetables. Store the remaining roasted vegetables with the 4 whole sausages in a large container.

14. Slice the bread loaf. In a freezer bag, place 8 slices from the center of the loaf (these will be used for the bruschetta), and place the other slices (those sliced nearest the ends of the loaf) in a separate freezer bag (these will be used with the eggplant caviar).

IT'S ALL DONE! LET COOL.

PLACE IN THE REFRIGERATOR:

* The eggplant caviar (keeps for 1 week)
* The marinated bell peppers (keeps for 1 week)
* The marinated chicken (keeps for 2 days)
* The roasted vegetables with the 4 cooked whole sausages (keeps for 3 days)
* The basil and cilantro, in an airtight container (keeps for 1 week)

PLACE IN THE FREEZER:

* The slices of bread
* The Spanish omelet, in its pan, covered with plastic wrap
* The container with the slices of green bell peppers, the cherry tomatoes, and the sausages

EACH NIGHT'S PREP

MONDAY

Main: Marinated chicken kebabs, durum wheat with roasted vegetables

Reheating time: 10 minutes

Cooking time: 15 minutes

Preparation time: 1 minute

Ingredients: the durum wheat, the marinated chicken, half the roasted vegetables, half the basil, salt, and pepper

Cook the wheat according to the package directions. Reheat the vegetables. Distribute the chicken pieces on 4 skewers (if using). Cook the skewers for 10 minutes in a skillet (or in the oven set on broil, or on an outdoor grill). Combine the vegetables and cooked wheat. Season with salt and pepper, and sprinkle with chopped basil. Serve with the chicken.

TUESDAY

Main: Merguez sausage, couscous

Reheating time: 10 minutes

Cooking time: 15 minutes

Preparation time: 1 minute

Ingredients: the couscous, the remaining roasted vegetables with the 4 whole sausages, ½ tsp ground coriander seeds, half the cilantro

Cook the couscous according to the package directions. In a skillet without added fat, reheat the sausages and set them aside. In the same skillet, place the vegetables, about ½ cup (120 mL) of water, and the ground coriander seeds. Let cook for 5 minutes. Chop the cilantro. Serve the vegetables and sausages with the couscous, sprinkled with cilantro.

For Wednesday, remove the omelet and the bag with the bread slices taken from the ends of the loaf from the freezer and thaw them in the refrigerator.

WEDNESDAY

Appetizer: Eggplant caviar

Main: Spanish omelet

Reheating time: 15 minutes

Ingredients: the omelet, three-fourths of the eggplant caviar, the slices of bread (the bag with the slices taken from the ends of the loaf), 2 sprigs of cilantro

Reheat the omelet in the oven preheated to 325°F (160°C). Toast the bread. Serve the toasted bread with the eggplant caviar, sprinkled with chopped cilantro. Place the remaining eggplant caviar in the refrigerator to use for the bruschetta on Thursday.

For Thursday, remove the bag with the 8 slices of bread from the freezer and thaw them in the refrigerator.

THURSDAY

Main: Summer bruschetta

Cooking time: 15 minutes

Preparation time: 7 minutes

Ingredients: the 8 slices of bread, the mozzarella, the remaining eggplant caviar, 16 strips of the marinated bell peppers, the bresaola, the bag of arugula, 2 sprigs of basil, olive oil

Preheat the oven to 400°F (200°C). Toast the bread in the oven for 4 minutes. Cut the mozzarella into 16 small slices. On each slice of bread, spread 1 tbsp of eggplant caviar, top with 2 strips of bell pepper, and 2 slices of mozzarella. Place the toasts in the oven for 1 minute to melt the mozzarella, then top with some of the bresaola, arugula, and basil. Drizzle with olive oil.

For Friday, remove the container with the green bell peppers, cherry tomatoes, and sausages from the freezer and thaw it in the refrigerator.

FRIDAY

Appetizer: Bell peppers marinated in garlic and olive oil

Main: Tunisian spaghetti

Reheating time: 15 minutes

Cooking time: 15 minutes

Preparation time: 5 minutes

Ingredients: the marinated green bell peppers, the remaining basil, the spaghetti noodles, the container with the thawed green bell peppers, tomatoes, and sausages, the cilantro, salt, and pepper

Remove the bell peppers from the marinade, sprinkle with the basil, season with salt and pepper, and serve.

Cook the spaghetti noodles to al dente (still firm to the bite). In a sauté pan, reheat the marinade from the green bell peppers. Add the vegetable and sausage mixture. Add the cooked spaghetti noodles, and sprinkle with the chopped cilantro. Toss to combine, and serve.

MENU #4

SHOPPING LIST   MENU #4

FRUITS / VEGETABLES

* 4 zucchini
* 1 large pineapple
* 3 avocados (ripe by Friday)
* 2 cucumbers
* 3 tomatoes (not too ripe)
* 2 cups (9 oz/250 g) shelled peas
* 1 head Bibb lettuce
* 1 small lemon
* 2 bunches green onions
* 1 bunch mint
* 6 garlic cloves
* 1 (2-in./5-cm) knob fresh ginger

PANTRY AND STAPLES

* 7 oz (200 g) farfalle pasta
* 2½ cups (9 oz/250 g) all-purpose flour
* ¾ cup (5¼ oz/150 g) brown rice
* 2½ tsp (⅓ oz/10 g) baking powder
* Herbes de Provence
* Soy sauce
* Ketchup
* Cornstarch
* Olive oil
* Salt, black pepper

MEAT / FISH

* 20 frozen raw, peeled shrimp
* 5¼ oz (150 g) diced ham*
* 1 (5¼-oz/150-g) smoked salmon fillet
  For a pork-free menu, replace the ham with turkey breast.

COLD CASE

* 6 large eggs
* 14 oz (400 g) Greek yogurt
* 1 (9-in./23-cm) piecrust
* 3⅓ cups (800 mL) heavy cream
* 1 wheel aged goat cheese (3½ to 5¼ oz/100 to 150 g), diced
* 1½ tbsp (1 oz/25 g) unsalted butter, for greasing the pan

DRY AND CANNED GOODS

* 4 hamburger buns
* 1 (15-oz/425-g) can corn
* Canned tuna (about 9 oz/250 g drained)
* 1 (15-oz/425-g) can chickpeas
* 1 (7-oz/200-g) jar artichoke hearts

MENUS

MONDAY

Appetizer: Zucchini gazpacho

Main: Tuna and tomato quiche

TUESDAY

Shrimp and pineapple fried rice

WEDNESDAY

Appetizer: Tzatziki sauce

Main: Zucchini and ham loaf*

THURSDAY

Chickpea burgers

FRIDAY

Farfalle and smoked salmon salad

For a pork-free menu, replace the ham with turkey breast.

SET UP

If you have enough work space, set out all the ingredients needed for this cooking session. This includes everything except the avocados, 2 tomatoes, the lemon, 1 garlic clove, the pasta, the frozen shrimp, smoked salmon, Greek yogurt, hamburger buns, corn, and artichoke hearts. This allows you to have everything at your fingertips and to not lose time searching for the ingredients in the pantry or refrigerator.

SET OUT THE NECESSARY EQUIPMENT:

* 1 (8-in./20-cm) tart pan
* Ceramic pie weights (or dried beans)
* 1 grater with large holes
* 1 colander
* 1 large mixing bowl
* 1 loaf pan
* 1 skillet
* 1 large saucepan
* 1 food processor
* 1 immersion blender
* 1 garlic press (if available)
* 1 salad spinner (or large bowl and clean kitchen towel)
* 5 containers: 1 large + 2 medium + 2 small
* 1 (6-cup/1.5-L-capacity) glass jar (for storing the zucchini gazpacho)
* Paper towels, parchment paper, aluminum foil

EVERYTHING IS NOW READY FOR A COOKING TIME OF 2 HOURS AND 10 MINUTES!

1. Preheat the oven to 350°F (180°C). Grease the tart pan. Line the pan with the piecrust, gently pressing the dough down into the pan and up the sides. Trim off any excess dough from around the edges, level with the top of the pan. Prick the bottom of the crust all over with a fork. Crumple the parchment paper included in the package with the piecrust (or use parchment paper), place it on top of the piecrust in the pan, then fill the pan with

the pie weights. Prebake the crust for 30 minutes, or until pale golden.

2. Peel the cucumbers, halve them lengthwise, and scrape out the seeds. Coarsely grate the flesh. Place the grated cucumber in a colander, season generously with salt, and set aside to drain while you continue cooking.

3. Cut off and discard the root ends of the green onions, strip off the first layer of skin, thinly slice the onions, and place them in a bowl.

4. Prepare the filling for the quiche: In the large mixing bowl, whisk 3 eggs with 1⅔ cups (400 mL) of cream until well combined. Whisk in 1 tsp of salt and a little pepper, until combined. Add 2 tbsp of the sliced onions, all of the tuna, and one-third of the peas. Wash 1 tomato and slice it into rounds. Scrape the filling into the bottom of the tart pan with the prebaked crust, and top it with the tomato slices. Bake for 45 minutes, or until golden on top, on a rack positioned near the top of the oven. Wash the mixing bowl.

5. In the large saucepan, bring 2 cups (480 mL) of salted water to a boil.

6. Peel 5 of the garlic cloves and press them through a garlic press (or mince them). Set them aside in a small bowl. Wash the zucchini. Cut 3 of the zucchini into large dice, and 1 into small dice.

7. To the saucepan of boiling water, add the large pieces of zucchini, and let cook for 10 minutes.

8. Rinse the lettuce. Detach the leaves and place them in the salad spinner (or large bowl) filled with water. Place any large damaged leaves in the saucepan with the zucchini. Gently spin the leaves dry (or use the kitchen towel), then place them in the large airtight container between two paper towels; the leaves will keep for up to 1 week.

9. Wash and gently dry the mint. Finely chop the entire bunch, and place it in a bowl.

10. In the saucepan with the zucchini, add 2 tbsp of chopped onion, ½ tsp chopped garlic, 1 tbsp of chopped mint, and just over ¾ cup (180 mL)

of cream. Blend thoroughly using the immersion blender. Transfer the gazpacho to the glass jar.

11. In the skillet over medium-high heat, heat 1 tbsp (15 mL) of olive oil until warm. Add 2 tbsp of chopped onions, ½ tsp of chopped garlic, the small diced zucchini, and ½ tsp of salt. Let cook for 10 minutes, uncovered, or until all of the liquid has evaporated. Let cool.

12. Prepare the loaf batter: In the large mixing bowl, lightly beat the remaining eggs with 3 tbsp (45 mL) of olive oil, and the remaining cream. Add the flour a little at a time, then add the baking powder, and stir with a whisk to thoroughly combine. Add the diced ham, goat cheese (diced), 1 tbsp of chopped mint, the cooked zucchini mixture, 1 tsp of salt, and 1 tbsp of herbes de Provence.

13. Scrape the batter into the greased loaf pan, and bake on a rack positioned near the bottom of the oven for 1 hour, or until a toothpick inserted in the center comes out with just a few moist

crumbs. After 10 minutes of baking time, make a shallow incision lengthwise down the center of the cake so that it rises evenly.

14. Rinse the brown rice and cook it according to the package directions. Drain.

15. Prepare the chickpea burgers: In the food processor, place the chickpeas (drained), 1 tbsp of chopped onions, a little chopped garlic, 1 tsp (5 mL) of olive oil, and 2 tbsp (¾ oz/20 g) of cornstarch. Process just until the mixture comes together to form a ball. Shape 4 round patties the diameter of the hamburger buns. Cook the patties for 2 minutes on each side in the skillet over high heat with a little oil. Remove the patties and set them aside.

16. Using a long serrated knife (such as a bread knife), halve the pineapple lengthwise. Using a small knife, cut all around the inside edge of the pineapple down through the flesh, being careful not to pierce the skin. Slice the flesh crosswise from top and bottom, moving from the outside edge to the

PLACE IN THE REFRIGERATOR:

* The remaining chopped green onions (keeps for 1 week)
* The remaining chopped mint (keeps for 1 week)
* The drained, grated cucumber (keeps for 1 week)
* The rinsed lettuce leaves (keeps for 1 week)
* The zucchini gazpacho (keeps for 2 days)
* The tuna quiche in its pan (keeps for 2 days)
* The empty pineapple halves, on a plate covered with foil (keeps for 4 days)
* The fried rice (keeps for 3 days)
* The chickpea patties (keeps for 5 days)

PLACE IN THE FREEZER:

* The zucchini and ham loaf, in its pan

fibrous core. Using a spoon, scoop out the flesh, and discard the fibrous core. Dice the flesh.

17. In the skillet, heat 1 tbsp (15 mL) of olive oil until warm. Add half the remaining chopped onions, all of the remaining chopped garlic, and the remaining peas. Grate the ginger over the top of the mixture. Add 1 tbsp (15 mL) of soy sauce. Let cook for 2 minutes, then add the diced pineapple and the rice, and cook for 5 more minutes.

EACH NIGHT'S PREP

MONDAY

Appetizer: Zucchini gazpacho

Main: Tuna and tomato quiche

Reheating time: 10 minutes

Ingredients: the gazpacho, the quiche, several lettuce leaves

Serve the gazpacho chilled. Reheat the quiche for 10 minutes in the oven preheated to 350°F (180°C). Serve with the lettuce leaves on the side.

TUESDAY

Main: Shrimp and pineapple fried rice

Cooking and reheating time: 10 minutes

Preparation time: 1 minute

Ingredients: olive oil, the frozen shrimp, the fried rice, the pineapple halves, the remaining chopped onions

In a skillet or sauté pan, heat 1 tbsp (15 mL) of olive oil until warm. Heat the shrimp for 2 minutes on each side, seasoned with a little salt. Add the fried rice, and reheat it for 5 minutes. Spoon the mixture into the pineapple halves. Sprinkle with the chopped green onion.

For Wednesday, remove the zucchini and ham loaf from the freezer and thaw it in the refrigerator.

WEDNESDAY

Appetizer: Tzatziki sauce

Main: Zucchini and ham loaf

Reheating time: 15 minutes

Preparation time: 5 minutes

Ingredients: two-thirds of the grated cucumbers, the Greek yogurt, the remaining chopped mint, the remaining garlic clove, the juice of half the lemon, the loaf, salt, and pepper

Make the tzatziki sauce: In a large serving bowl, combine the grated cucumbers, yogurt, mint, garlic clove (very finely chopped or pressed through a garlic press), lemon juice, and salt and pepper. Set aside 4 tbsp of the tzatziki sauce in a bowl in the refrigerator; this will be used for the sauce on the hamburgers for tomorrow. Wrap the remaining lemon half in plastic wrap and refrigerate. Reheat the loaf in the oven preheated to 350°F (180°C). Unmold, and serve.

THURSDAY

Main: Chickpea burgers

Reheating time: 5 minutes

Preparation time: 10 minutes

Ingredients: the hamburger buns, the chickpea patties, the ketchup, the remaining tzatziki sauce, 1 tomato, 4 lettuce leaves

Toast the hamburger buns under the oven broiler or in a toaster. Reheat the chickpea patties in a skillet. Slice the tomato into rounds. Cut the lettuce leaves into strips. Spread a little ketchup on top of each bottom bun, then place some lettuce strips on top, then a chickpea patty. Spread on 1 tbsp of tzatziki sauce, and top with 1 or 2 slices of tomatoes. Add the top bun, and serve.

FRIDAY

Main: Farfalle and smoked salmon salad

Cooking time: 15 minutes

Preparation time: 10 minutes

Ingredients: the pasta, the avocados, the remaining tomato, the salmon fillet, artichoke hearts, the remaining grated cucumber, the remaining lettuce, 3 tbsp (45 mL) of olive oil, the juice of the remaining lemon half, the corn, salt, and pepper

Cook the pasta according to the package directions. Meanwhile, dice the avocados, tomato, and salmon. Quarter the artichoke hearts. Cut the lettuce leaves into strips. Drain the pasta and rinse it under cold water. In a large bowl, vigorously whisk together the olive oil and lemon juice with a little salt and pepper. Add all the ingredients and stir to combine.

FALL

MENU #1

FRUITS / VEGETABLES

* 1 large (3⅓ to 4½-lb/1.5 to 2-kg) butternut squash (or other winter squash)
* 6 carrots
* 1 celery stalk
* 3⅓ lb (1.5 kg) Charlotte potatoes (or similar waxy salad potato)
* 1 large bag field lettuce (about 9 oz/250 g), sell-by date > 3 or 4 days
* 1 large bag prewashed spinach leaves or baby spinach (about 9 oz/250 g)
* 1 bunch flat-leaf parsley
* 1 bunch cilantro
* 2 garlic cloves
* 5 yellow onions
* 1 small lemon
* 1 lime
* 1 (1-in./3-cm) knob fresh ginger
* 1 bunch green onions (aka scallions)
* 1 small cucumber
* 2 small fresh red chile peppers (such as tabasco) or ¼ tsp ground red pepper
* 1 small Granny Smith or Golden Delicious apple, according to your tastes, preferably organic

PANTRY AND STAPLES

* 16 oz (454 g) small pasta shells
* 2 bay leaves
* Dried bread crumbs
* Balsamic vinegar
* Olive oil
* Ground cumin
* Salt, black pepper

MEAT / FISH

* 5¼ oz (150 g) smoked lardons (thick-cut cubed bacon) or 2 blocks (7 oz/200 g) smoked tofu
* 3 beef cheeks (to save time have the butcher cut them into small pieces) or other cuts of beef stew meat (such as chuck)
* 1 package beef carpaccio (about 7 oz/200 g) sell-by date > 6 days

COLD CASE

* 2 cups (480 mL) heavy cream
* 1 cup (4 oz/113 g) grated Parmesan cheese

DRY AND CANNED GOODS

* 1 (15-oz/425-g) can chickpeas
* Tahini (ground sesame paste) or sesame oil (optional)
* 4 pita breads
* ⅔ cup (3½ oz/100 g) unsalted cashews
* 1⅓ cups (9 oz/250 g) jasmine rice
* 1 small jar whole chestnuts
* 2 cans (about 1¾ lb/800 g) crushed tomatoes
* Scant ½ cup (100 mL) red wine
* 7 oz (200 g) rice stick noodles (rice vermicelli)
* 2 beef bouillon cubes
* 2 star anise pods
* 1 small jar nuoc mam (fish sauce)

MENUS

MONDAY

Pasta with beef cheek sauce

TUESDAY

Appetizer: Hummus with dipping vegetables and pita bread

Main: Butternut-chestnut soup with lardons*

WEDNESDAY

Appetizer: Field lettuce, green apple, and cashew salad

Main: Shepherd's pie

THURSDAY

Butternut squash and spinach fried rice, toasted cashews

FRIDAY

Pho

For a pork-free menu, replace the lardons with smoked tofu.

SET UP

If you have enough work space, set out all the ingredients needed for this cooking session. This includes everything except the field lettuce, lime, apple, lardons, carpaccio, pita breads, pasta, rice noodles, nuoc mam, and vinegar. This allows you to have everything at your fingertips and to not lose time searching for the ingredients in the pantry or refrigerator.

SET OUT THE NECESSARY EQUIPMENT:

* 1 lidded Dutch oven (preferably oven safe)
* 1 large gratin baking dish (or shallow baking dish)
* 1 large stockpot (or 1 very large saucepan) for cooking the potatoes
* 2 large saucepans
* 1 baking sheet
* 1 sauté pan or 1 large skillet
* 1 immersion blender
* 1 blender or food processor (for puréeing the chickpeas for the hummus)
* 1 salad spinner (or large bowl and clean kitchen towel)
* 1 food mill (or potato masher)
* 1 large glass container (for storing the raw vegetable sticks)
* 1 (6-cup/1.5-L-capacity) glass jar (for storing the pho broth)
* 2 small lidded glass jars
* 3 containers: 2 large + 1 medium
* 1 large serving bowl for the hummus
* Paper towels (or 1 thin clean and dry kitchen towel)
* Plastic wrap

EVERYTHING IS NOW READY FOR A COOKING TIME OF 2 HOURS!

1. Preheat the oven to 350°F (180°C).
2. Peel and chop the yellow onions. Set aside one-third of the onions in a container. Peel the carrots.

Cut 3 of the carrots into small dice, and cut the other 3 into sticks. Peel the cucumber and cut it into sticks. Refrigerate the vegetable sticks in an airtight container: these will be served for dipping in the hummus. Cut the celery stalk into small dice.

3. In the Dutch oven, heat 4 tbsp (60 mL) of olive oil until warm. Add two-thirds of the chopped onions, the diced carrots, and the diced celery stalk. Season with salt, and let cook for 5 minutes over medium heat. Add the pieces of beef cheek and brown them on all sides. Add the red wine, and cook for a few minutes longer, until the liquid is slightly reduced. Add 1 chopped fresh chile pepper (or the ground red pepper) and the bay leaves; season with salt. Stir to combine, then add the crushed tomatoes. Cover the pot, then place it in the oven (note: if you are using a pot that is not oven safe, continue cooking on the stovetop). Let simmer while you are finishing the remaining cooking, checking from time to time that the meat remains immersed in the liquid.

4. Fill the large stockpot with salted water and bring to a boil. Peel the potatoes and cook them in the large stockpot for about 20 minutes, or just until tender when pierced with a fork.

5. Rinse the rice and cook it in boiling water in the large saucepan until still somewhat firm to the bite.

6. Meanwhile, place the cashews on the baking sheet and toast them for 5 minutes on a rack placed near the top of the oven, stirring halfway through the cooking time. Once cooled, place them in a small jar.

7. Peel the garlic cloves and finely chop them. Set them aside.

8. Drain the rice and let it cool. Rinse the saucepan, fill it with fresh water, and heat it to make the soup.

9. Peel the butternut squash. Cut it lengthwise in half and scrape out the seeds. Cut the flesh into small dice. Set aside one-fourth of the diced flesh for the

fried rice, and place the remaining in the saucepan of boiling water and let cook for 20 minutes.

10. Prepare the herbs: Remove any rubber bands from around the stems of the cilantro and parsley and immerse the herbs in the salad spinner filled with water (or use a large bowl). Drain the water, then gently spin the herbs dry (or use the clean kitchen towel); the herbs should be as dry as possible so they stay fresh. Place the herbs in an airtight container between two sheets of paper towels (or wrapped in the kitchen towel).

11. Cut off the root ends of the green onions, strip off the first layer of skin, then thinly slice the onions. Place them in a small glass jar.

12. Drain the potatoes and process them through the food mill (or potato masher). Add 1 cup (240 mL) of the cream, half the grated Parmesan, and a little chopped garlic. Stir to thoroughly combine, and set aside.

13. Drain about half the cooking water from the butternut squash, then blend the squash with the

immersion blender with the remaining cooking water, the remaining cream, the chestnuts, and some salt and pepper. Wash the immersion blender.

14. Prepare the broth for the pho in the saucepan: Peel and slice the ginger. Bring 6 cups (1.5 L) of water to a boil with the bouillon cubes, the star anise pods, the ginger, and a little piece of chile pepper. Allow the broth to boil for 5 minutes, remove the chile pepper, and set the broth aside to cool.

15. In the sauté pan, brown the remaining chopped onions and half the chopped garlic in a little olive oil. Add the remaining cubes of butternut squash. Once the squash pieces begin to brown, add a ladle of the pho broth. Cover, and let cook for 10 minutes over low heat. Add the spinach and cook just until wilted. Add the cooked rice, and immediately turn off the heat. Let cool.

16. Prepare the hummus: In the blender, blend the chickpeas (drained) with the juice of the lemon,

1 tbsp (15 g) of tahini (if using), 1 tsp of cumin, the remaining chopped garlic, 2 tbsp (30 mL) of olive oil (or use sesame oil if you do not have tahini), and some salt and pepper. Transfer the mixture to the large serving bowl.

17. Remove the pot from the oven, remove half the meat and sauce, and transfer them to the baking dish; roughly blend the contents of the baking dish using the immersion blender. Place the pot back in the oven until the cooking session is complete. Spread the mashed potatoes over the meat mixture, and sprinkle the top with the dried bread crumbs. Place the baking dish on a rack near the top of the oven, and bake for about 10 minutes (the dish will finish cooking when it's reheated prior to serving).

IT'S ALL DONE! LET COOL.

PLACE IN THE REFRIGERATOR:

* The pot with the beef cheek sauce (keeps for 2 days)
* The pot with the butternut-chestnut soup, if you are serving it within 2 days
* The hummus (keeps for 5 days)
* The vegetable sticks (keeps for 5 days)
* The herbs (keeps for 1 week)

PLACE IN THE FREEZER:

* The butternut-chestnut soup, if you are serving it more than 2 days after preparing it
* The pho broth in the glass jar (be sure to leave a little space at the top of the jar)
* The fried rice
* The shepherd's pie, in its dish, covered with plastic wrap
* The chopped green onions

PANTRY:

* The toasted cashews

EACH NIGHT'S PREP

MONDAY

Main: Pasta with beef cheek sauce

Reheating time: 15 minutes

Cooking time: 15 minutes

Preparation time: 2 minutes

Ingredients: the beef cheek sauce, the pasta shells, the remaining grated Parmesan, 4 sprigs flat-leaf parsley, salt, and pepper

Reheat the beef cheek sauce. Meanwhile, cook the pasta according to the package directions.

Serve the pasta covered with the beef cheek sauce. Sprinkle the Parmesan on top, then a few leaves of chopped parsley. Season with salt and pepper.

For Tuesday, if you have frozen the butternut-chestnut soup, remove it from the freezer and thaw it in the refrigerator.

TUESDAY

Appetizer: Hummus with dipping vegetables and pita bread

Main: Butternut-chestnut soup with lardons (or smoked tofu)

Reheating time: 10 minutes

Cooking time: 5 minutes

Preparation time: 5 minutes

Ingredients: 2 sprigs of cilantro, the hummus, the pita breads, the butternut-chestnut soup, the lardons (or smoked tofu), the carrot and cucumber sticks, salt, and pepper

Chop the cilantro and sprinkle it over the hummus. Heat the pita breads in the toaster. Reheat the soup. In a skillet, brown the lardons (or smoked tofu) in a little olive oil, and divide them among the soup bowls. Serve the vegetable sticks with the hummus and toasted pita breads as an appetizer and the soup as the main.

For Wednesday, remove the shepherd's pie from the freezer and thaw it in the refrigerator.

WEDNESDAY

Appetizer: Field lettuce, green apple, and cashew salad

Main: Shepherd's pie

Reheating time: 15 minutes

Preparation time: 5 minutes

Ingredients: the apple, 3 tbsp (45 mL) of olive oil, 1 tbsp (15 mL) of balsamic vinegar, the bag of field lettuce, 4 sprigs of parsley or cilantro (or a mixture of the two), half the toasted cashews, the shepherd's pie, salt, and pepper

Wash and core the apple and slice it into sticks. In the bottom of a large bowl, vigorously whisk together the oil and vinegar. Season with salt and pepper. Add the lettuce, apple sticks, and herbs and toss to coat. Sprinkle the cashews over the top. Reheat the shepherd's pie in the oven preheated to 350°F (180°C).

For Thursday, remove the fried rice from the freezer and thaw it in the refrigerator.

THURSDAY

Main: Butternut squash and spinach fried rice, toasted cashews

Reheating time: 10 minutes

Preparation time: 1 minute

Ingredients: the fried rice, the remaining cashews, 4 sprigs cilantro

Reheat the fried rice, then sprinkle it with the toasted cashews and chopped cilantro.

For Friday, remove the pho broth and the chopped green onions from the freezer and thaw them in the refrigerator.

FRIDAY

Main: Pho

Cooking time: 5 minutes

Preparation time: 5 minutes

Ingredients: the thawed broth, the rice stick noodles, the thawed chopped green onions, the beef carpaccio, the lime, 4 tbsp (60 mL) nuoc mam, the remaining cilantro

In a saucepan, bring the broth to a boil, then remove it from heat. Add the noodles and cook for the amount of time indicated on the package. Meanwhile, slice the carpaccio into thin strips. Place the strips in the broth, add the juice from the lime, the nuoc mam, the onions, and the chopped cilantro.

MENU #2

SHOPPING CART MENU #2

SHOPPING LIST   MENU #2

FRUITS / VEGETABLES

* 3 medium sweet potatoes
* 2¼ lb (1 kg) Charlotte potatoes (or similar waxy salad potato)
* 1 large head cauliflower
* 1 small bag arugula (about 5 oz/140 g), sell-by date > 4 or 5 days after purchase
* 1 large bag shredded cabbage (about 9 oz/250 g), or a mixture of shredded cabbage and carrots, sell-by date > 4 or 5 days
* 1 small container cherry tomatoes (about 6 oz/170 g)
* 1 bunch flat-leaf parsley
* 1 bunch chives
* 8 garlic cloves
* 2 yellow onions
* 1 small organic lemon
* 1 (2-in./5-cm) knob fresh ginger
* 18 oz (500 g) small white button mushrooms

PANTRY AND STAPLES

* 1 lb (454 g) linguine (or spaghetti noodles)
* 1 small jar tomato sauce (about 10 oz/280 g)
* Curry powder
* Whole nutmeg
* Herbes de Provence
* Mustard
* Olive oil
* Salt, black pepper

MEAT / FISH

* About 12 pieces cooked, peeled shrimp (sell-by date > 1 or 2 days)
* 14 oz (400 g) boneless, skinless chicken breasts
* 4 slices ham (or sliced cooked turkey breast)
* 14 oz (400 g) cod loin (fresh or frozen)

COLD CASE

* 2 cups (480 mL) heavy cream
* 2 cups (16 oz/454 g) crème fraîche
* 4 cups (1 L) whole milk
* 6 large eggs
* 1 small container fresh mini mozzarella cheese balls (about 4½ oz/125 g drained)
* 2 tbsp (1 oz/30 g) unsalted butter
* 1 cup (4 oz/113 g) grated Parmesan cheese
* 1 small container Parmesan cheese shavings (about 4 oz/113 g), or 1 small wedge Parmesan cheese to make shavings

DRY AND CANNED GOODS

* 1 cup (7 oz/200 g) basmati or light brown rice
* 1½ cups (9 oz/250 g) instant polenta (cornmeal)
* 1 can crushed tomatoes (about 14 oz/400 g)
* 1⅔ to 2 cups (400 to 480 mL) coconut milk
* ½ cup (1¾ oz/50 g) walnut halves

MENUS

MONDAY

Appetizer: Cauliflower velouté soup with sautéed shrimp

Main: Polenta pizza with mushrooms

TUESDAY

Sweet potato* and chicken curry

WEDNESDAY

Cauliflower and potato gratin with ham**

THURSDAY

Appetizer: Cabbage, boiled egg, and cherry tomato salad with creamy dressing

Main: Linguine with garlic cream, arugula, walnuts, and Parmesan shavings

FRIDAY

Fresh cod and sweet potato* shepherd's pie

If you do not like sweet potatoes, replace half the quantity with carrots (for the curry) and the other half with potatoes (for the shepherd's pie), and follow the instructions exactly as written.

**For a pork-free menu, replace the ham with turkey breast.

SET UP

If you have enough work space, set out all the ingredients needed for this cooking session. This includes everything except the arugula, shredded cabbage, cherry tomatoes, shrimp, Parmesan shavings, rice, and pasta. This allows you to have everything at your fingertips and to not lose time searching for the ingredients in the pantry or refrigerator.

SET OUT THE NECESSARY EQUIPMENT:

* 2 small gratin baking dishes (or shallow baking dishes)
* 1 skillet
* 1 large stockpot (or very large saucepan) for cooking the cauliflower
* 1 large steam cooker or lidded stockpot with a steam basket
* 1 small bowl
* 1 large mixing bowl
* 1 baking sheet
* 1 small saucepan
* 1 sauté pan
* 1 small grater or zester (for the lemon zest and nutmeg)
* 1 immersion blender
* 1 salad spinner (or large bowl)
* 1 clean kitchen towel
* 1 food mill (or potato masher)
* 2 (6-cup/1.5-L-capacity) glass jars (for storing the garlic cream and the cauliflower velouté soup)
* 1 small lidded jar
* 5 containers: 2 large + 3 small
* Paper towels (or clean and dry thin kitchen towel)
* Parchment paper, plastic wrap, aluminum foil

EVERYTHING IS NOW READY FOR A COOKING TIME OF 2 HOURS AND 10 MINUTES!

1. Fill the stockpot with salted water and bring it to a simmer. Wash the cauliflower and cut it into

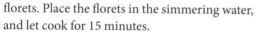

florets. Place the florets in the simmering water, and let cook for 15 minutes.

2. Peel the sweet potatoes and the Charlotte potatoes. Cut the sweet potatoes into large dice, and slice the Charlotte potatoes into thin rounds. Place the potato cubes and rounds together in the steam cooker, with the cubes on the bottom and the rounds on top. Let cook for about 15 minutes; they should remain somewhat firm.

3. Preheat the oven to 400°F (200°C). Drain the cauliflower. Remove half the cauliflower, and blend it with the immersion blender with just over ¾ cup (200 mL) of the cream. Add a little water (about ¾ cup/200 mL) to obtain a smooth, creamy consistency. Season with salt and pepper. Transfer the mixture to a jar. Roughly blend the remaining cauliflower and combine it with 3 tbsp (1½ oz/44 g) of crème fraîche, a little freshly grated nutmeg, and salt and pepper. Cut the ham slices into squares and stir to combine them into the mixture.

4. At this point, the potato rounds should be cooked. Remove half of them, and place them in the bottom of a baking dish. Pour the cauliflower-ham mixture over the top of the potatoes. Top with one-fourth of the grated Parmesan, and bake for 20 minutes, or until browned and bubbling. Rinse and dry the stockpot.

5. Place the cod in a separate baking dish. Season with salt, and precook it for 3 minutes (5 minutes if frozen) in the microwave (or in the oven for double the amount of time).

6. Meanwhile, wash the chives and parsley by immersing them in a large volume of cold water, then gently dry them in the clean kitchen towel or in the salad spinner. Chop three-fourths of the chives and place them in the small bowl. Place the parsley and remaining chives in an airtight container between two sheets of paper towels.

7. Drain the cooking liquid from the cod, and crumble the cod into the bottom of the baking dish. Add 3 tbsp (1½ oz/44 g) of crème fraîche,

the chopped chives, a little grated zest from the lemon, and season with a little pepper. Stir to combine.

8. Place the eggs in the small saucepan filled with water and cook them for 8 minutes after the water begins to boil.

9. Using the food mill (or potato masher), in the large mixing bowl, mash the remaining cooked potato rounds with half the cooked sweet potatoes. Add the remaining crème fraîche, season with salt and pepper, and stir to combine. Spread this mixture on top of the cod. Bake for 15 minutes, or just until the cod is cooked through.

10. At this point, the eggs should be cooked. Rinse them under cold water to stop the cooking, and refrigerate them for up to 5 days.

11. Prepare the polenta: In the stockpot, place the whole milk and ½ tsp of salt. Bring the milk to a simmer, and sprinkle the polenta into the pan. Reduce the heat, and let cook for 1 minute while whisking constantly. Add the butter and the

remaining grated Parmesan. Stir to combine, and let cool slightly.

12. Meanwhile, peel and chop the garlic cloves and the onions. Cut off and discard the mushroom stems, and gently wash and dry the tops. Cut the tops in half or into quarters, depending on their size.

13. In the skillet, heat 2 tbsp (30 mL) of olive oil, and add the equivalent of 2 chopped garlic cloves, the mushrooms, and ½ tsp of salt. Let cook for 5 minutes over medium heat, just until the mushrooms are no longer releasing any liquid. At the end of the cooking time, chop half the parsley and sprinkle it over the mushrooms.

14. Meanwhile, line a baking sheet with parchment paper and spread the cooled polenta out into a ½-in. (1.5-cm)-thick oval. Spread the tomato sauce over the top of the polenta, leaving a ¾-in. (2-cm) border, then distribute the mozzarella balls and the cooked parsley and mushrooms over the top. Sprinkle on 1 tbsp of the herbes de

Provence. Bake for 5 minutes, or until the cheese is melted.

15. In the sauté pan, heat 2 tbsp (30 mL) of olive oil until warm. Add one-fourth of the remaining chopped garlic, the chopped onions, some salt, and 1 tbsp of curry powder. Let cook for 5 minutes, or until browned. Peel and chop the ginger. Add three-fourths of the ginger to the pan. Place the remaining ginger and one-fourth of the remaining garlic in an airtight container and refrigerate. Cut the chicken breasts into cubes, and brown them in the pan. Add the crushed tomatoes and the coconut milk. Let simmer for 15 minutes.

16. Meanwhile, toast the walnuts in the warm oven (turned off) for 5 minutes. In the skillet, heat 2 tbsp (30 mL) of olive oil until warm, and cook the remaining chopped garlic with ½ tsp of salt. Cook for 2 minutes, or until lightly browned, then add just over ¾ cup (200 mL) of cream. Let cook for 2 minutes, then transfer the mixture to the jar. Place the walnuts in the small jar.

17. Prepare the creamy dressing for the cabbage salad: In a small container, vigorously whisk together 1 tsp (5 mL) of mustard, ½ tsp of salt, and the juice and remaining zest of the lemon while adding the remaining cream a little at a time, until smooth. Add the remaining sweet potatoes to the chicken curry.

IT'S ALL DONE! LET COOL.

PLACE IN THE REFRIGERATOR:

* The cauliflower velouté soup in the large jar, leaving a little air at the top (keeps for 2 days)
* The polenta pizza, preferably on the baking sheet, covered with foil (keeps for 2 days)
* The sweet potato and chicken curry (keeps for 2 days)
* The hard-boiled eggs (keeps for 5 days)
* The creamy dressing (keeps for 10 days)
* The remaining parsley and chives (keeps for 10 days)
* The chopped garlic and ginger mixture (keeps for 10 days)

PLACE IN THE FREEZER:

* The sweet potato and chicken curry, if you are serving it more than 2 days after preparing it
* The cauliflower and potato gratin, in its baking dish, covered with plastic wrap
* The garlic cream
* The cod and sweet potato shepherd's pie, in its baking dish, covered with plastic wrap

PANTRY:

* The toasted walnuts

EACH NIGHT'S PREP

MONDAY

Appetizer: Cauliflower velouté soup with sautéed shrimp

Main: Polenta pizza with mushrooms

Reheating time: 10 minutes

Cooking time: 2 minutes

Preparation time: 2 minutes

Ingredients: the polenta pizza, the cauliflower velouté soup, 1 tbsp (15 mL) olive oil, the garlic-ginger mixture, 3 sprigs parsley, the peeled shrimp, salt, and pepper

Reheat the polenta pizza in the oven preheated to 325°F (160°C). Reheat the cauliflower velouté soup in a saucepan while stirring. In a small skillet, heat the olive oil. Add the chopped garlic and ginger. Chop the parsley and sprinkle it over the shrimp. Add the shrimp to the skillet and cook for 1 to 2 minutes. Top each bowl of velouté soup with some of this mixture and serve.

For Tuesday, if the sweet potato and chicken curry is frozen, remove it from the freezer and thaw it in the refrigerator.

TUESDAY

Main: Sweet potato and chicken curry

Reheating time: 15 minutes

Cooking time: 10 minutes

Preparation time: 3 minutes

Ingredients: the sweet potato and chicken curry, the rice, the remaining chives

Reheat the curry. Thoroughly rinse the rice and cook it according to the package directions. Serve it on the side with a sprinkle of chives.

For Wednesday, remove the cauliflower and potato gratin from the freezer and thaw it in the refrigerator.

WEDNESDAY

Main: Cauliflower and potato gratin with ham (or turkey)

Reheating time: 15 minutes

Ingredients: the cauliflower and potato gratin

Reheat the gratin in the oven preheated to 300°F (150°C) and serve.

For Thursday, remove the garlic cream from the freezer and thaw it in the refrigerator.

THURSDAY

Appetizer: Cabbage, boiled egg, and cherry tomato salad with creamy dressing

Main: Linguine with garlic cream, arugula, walnuts, and Parmesan shavings

Reheating time: 5 minutes

Cooking time: 15 minutes

Preparation time: 10 minutes

Ingredients: the linguine, the thawed garlic cream, the hard-boiled eggs, the cherry tomatoes, the shredded cabbage, the remaining parsley, the creamy dressing, the bag of arugula, the toasted walnuts, the Parmesan shavings, olive oil, and pepper

Cook the pasta according to the package directions. Reheat the garlic cream.

Meanwhile, peel the hard-boiled eggs and cut them into quarters. Cut the cherry tomatoes into quarters. Place the shredded cabbage in a large shallow serving dish, top with the cherry tomatoes and hard-boiled eggs. Sprinkle with the chopped parsley. Pour the creamy dressing over the top. Serve the noodles with the garlic cream, topped with the arugula, walnuts, and Parmesan shavings. Season with pepper and a drizzle of olive oil.

For Friday, remove the shepherd's pie from the freezer and thaw it in the refrigerator.

FRIDAY

Main: Fresh cod and sweet potato shepherd's pie

Reheating time: 15 minutes

Ingredients: the shepherd's pie

Reheat the shepherd's pie in the oven preheated to 325°F (160°C) and serve.

MENU #3

SHOPPING LIST MENU #3

FRUITS / VEGETABLES

* 1 Belgian endive
* 6 Charlotte potatoes (or similar waxy salad potato; 36 oz/170 g)
* 2¼ lb (1 kg) frozen chopped spinach
* 2 small quinces
* 2½ lb (1.2 kg) turnips (regular or golden ball)
* 4 carrots
* 2 leeks
* 1 bunch cilantro
* 1 bunch chives
* 5 garlic cloves
* 5 yellow onions
* 2 red onions
* 1 small organic lemon

PANTRY AND STAPLES

* ¾ cup (3 oz/80 g) all-purpose flour
* Potato starch or cornstarch
* 1 cup (7 oz/200 g) couscous
* 6 tbsp (120 g) honey
* Ground cumin
* Cinnamon (or quatre épices spice blend)
* Ras el hanout (Moroccan spice blend)
* Whole nutmeg
* Olive oil
* Salt, black pepper

MEAT / FISH

* 2¼ lb (1 kg) boneless lamb shoulder, cut into small pieces by your butcher
* 2 fresh skinless salmon fillets
* 4 slices smoked salmon
* 5¼ oz (150 g) lardons* (thick-cut bacon, cut into small cubes), or 7 oz (200 g) smoked tofu

    For a pork-free menu, replace the lardons with smoked tofu.

COLD CASE

* 4 cups (960 ml) whole milk
* 10½ oz (300 g) *fromage frais*, preferably St Môret brand (or a good ricotta, mascarpone, or plain yogurt)
* 1 small log fresh goat cheese (4¼ to 6⅓ oz/120 to 180 g)
* 1 (9-in./23-cm) piecrust
* 1 (9-oz/250-g) package fresh lasagna noodles
* 9 tbsp (4½ oz/125 g) unsalted butter
* 2 cups (480 mL) heavy cream

DRY AND CANNED GOODS

* 1 (5-oz/142-g) can tuna
* 1 (15-oz/425-g) can chickpeas

MENUS

MONDAY

Appetizer: Tuna rillettes endive bites

Main: Turnip, honey, and goat cheese tart Tatin

TUESDAY

Lamb tagine with quince

WEDNESDAY

Appetizer: Spinach and *fromage frais* velouté soup

Main: Potato, leek, onion, and lardons* gratin

THURSDAY

Lamb keftas, panfried carrots, turnips, and chickpeas with cumin

FRIDAY

Salmon and spinach lasagna

*For a pork-free menu, replace the lardons with smoked tofu.

SET UP

If you have enough work space, set out all the ingredients needed for this cooking session. This includes everything except the endive and the couscous. This allows you to have everything at your fingertips and to not lose time searching for the ingredients in the pantry or refrigerator.

SET OUT THE NECESSARY EQUIPMENT:

* 3 small bowls
* 2 large baking dishes
* 1 large sauté pan
* 1 large saucepan
* 1 medium saucepan
* 1 lidded Dutch oven or stockpot
* 1 (8-in./20-cm) tart pan
* 1 small grater or zester (for the lemon zest and nutmeg)
* 1 food processor (for grinding the lamb meat for the meatballs)
* 1 immersion blender

* 1 large microwave-safe bowl
* 1 large bowl (for the tuna rillettes)
* 1 (6-cup/1.5-L-capacity) glass jar (for storing the velouté soup)
* 2 containers: 1 large + 1 small
* Parchment paper, plastic wrap, aluminum foil, paper towels, airtight storage bag

EVERYTHING IS NOW READY FOR A COOKING TIME OF 2 HOURS!

1. Peel and roughly chop the yellow and red onions and the garlic cloves. Set them aside in separate bowls.

2. In the Dutch oven, melt 1 tbsp (¾ oz/20 g) of butter with 1 tbsp (15 mL) of olive oil. Add half the chopped onions, half the garlic cloves, ½ tsp of cumin, ½ tsp of cinnamon, and 1 tsp of salt. Let cook for 2 minutes, or until slightly softened. Add the pieces of lamb and 3 tbsp (60 g) of honey, stir, then add just over ¾ cup (200 mL) of water. Bring

to a boil, then lower the heat to its lowest setting and let simmer, covered, for 1 hour.

3. Meanwhile, peel the potatoes, turnips, carrots, and quinces. Thoroughly wash the leeks (including in between the leaves) and thinly slice them. Cut 3 of the potatoes into rounds, and 3 of them into large dice.

4. In the large sauté pan, heat 2 tbsp (30 mL) of olive oil, then add the remaining chopped onions, the sliced leeks, the potato rounds, and 1 tsp of salt. Let cook for 30 minutes, covered, stirring from time to time.

5. Prepare a béchamel sauce (it will be used for two of the recipes): In the large saucepan, gently melt 6 tbsp (3 oz/80 g) of butter, then add the flour. Stir with a wooden spoon, just until all of the butter is absorbed into the flour and the mixture forms a sort of paste. Pour in all of the milk at once. Let cook over medium heat while stirring constantly, just until the mixture thickens (about 10 minutes). Off the heat, season with 1 tsp of salt, a little

pepper, and a little grated nutmeg. Transfer the béchamel sauce to the large container.

6. Preheat the oven to 350°F (180°C). Wash the large saucepan, fill it halfway with salted water, and bring it to a boil. Meanwhile, cut the quinces into quarters. Remove and discard the fibrous core and the seeds, as if coring an apple.

7. As soon as the water begins to boil, add the whole turnips and let cook for 15 minutes. Chop the quinces into large pieces and set aside.

8. Transfer the panfried mixture of leeks, onion, and potatoes to a large baking dish. In the same sauté pan (do not rinse it), brown the lardons (or the smoked diced tofu) for 2 minutes over high heat. Add the lardons to the baking dish. Add the cream, and stir to thoroughly combine all the ingredients. Spread one-third of the béchamel sauce over the top. Bake for 30 minutes, or until golden on top and bubbling.

9. Drain the turnips and rinse them under cold water. Cut them into quarters. Add the quince

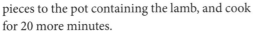

pieces to the pot containing the lamb, and cook for 20 more minutes.

10. Wash the large saucepan. Melt the remaining 2 tbsp (1 oz/25 g) of the butter with 1 tbsp (15 mL) of olive oil. Add the remaining honey and three-fourths of the turnips. Let cook for 15 minutes, covered, turning them once halfway through the cooking time. Let cook for 10 more minutes, uncovered, just until the liquid evaporates and the turnips are well caramelized.

11. While the turnips are cooking, place the chopped spinach in the microwave-safe bowl, and microwave it on low to thaw. Meanwhile, bring 1½ cups (360 mL) of salted water to a boil in the medium saucepan. Add the diced potatoes, and let cook for 10 minutes. Add one-third of the thawed spinach, and let cook for 5 minutes. Season the remaining chopped spinach with salt. Zest and juice the lemon, and set the zest and juice aside.

12. Line the bottom of the tart pan with a circle of parchment paper cut to the same diameter as the pan. Arrange the cooked turnips in the bottom of the tart pan, overlapping them snugly together, then crumble the goat cheese over the top. Drape the piecrust over the turnips, folding the edge of the dough down and inside the pan to form an attractive border. Prick the top of the dough several times with the tip of a knife to allow steam to escape while baking. Bake for 25 minutes, or until golden and flaky on top.

13. In the bottom of the separate large baking dish, spread a layer of the béchamel sauce. Cut up the salmon fillet steaks into medium-size pieces. Cover the sauce with a layer of the lasagna noodles. Cover the noodles with one-third of the remaining spinach. Top with pieces of salmon, then a crumbled slice of the smoked salmon, some lemon juice, and a little more béchamel sauce. Repeat these steps until all of the ingredients are used. Bake for 30 minutes, or until golden on top, on a rack set below the tart Tatin.

14. In the same pan used to cook the turnips (do not wash the pan), heat 2 tbsp (30 mL) of olive

oil, then add half the chopped red onions. Season with a little salt, and let cook until lightly browned. Meanwhile, cut the carrots into rounds. Add them to the pan with the remaining turnips and ½ tsp of cumin. Let cook for 20 minutes. At the end of the cooking time, add the chickpeas (drained), and stir to combine. Wash and gently dry the cilantro.

15. To the saucepan with the spinach and potatoes, add two-thirds (about 7 oz/200 g) of the *fromage frais* and 2 small pieces of chopped garlic. Using the immersion blender, blend for several minutes until smooth.

16. Remove the lamb, quince, and onions from the pot. Bring the cooking juices to a boil and let reduce slightly. Meanwhile, prepare the lamb keftas: Place half the lamb pieces in the food processor with the remaining chopped garlic and red onions, one-fourth of the cilantro, 1 tsp of salt, a little pepper, ½ tsp of ras el hanout, and 1 tbsp of potato starch. Pulse to combine, then shape the mixture into meatballs using your hands. In the

sauté pan, heat a little oil until warm, then cook the meatballs for 10 minutes, stirring frequently. Add the remaining lamb and quince to the pot with the reduced cooking juices. Add some chopped cilantro.

17. Make the tuna rillettes by combining the remaining *fromage frais* in the large bowl with the tuna (drained), chopped chives, and the lemon zest.

IT'S ALL DONE! LET COOL.

PLACE IN THE REFRIGERATOR:

* The tuna rillettes
* The tart Tatin, in its pan, covered with foil
* The lamb tagine, in its pot (keeps for 2 days)
* The remaining cilantro, rolled up in a paper towel and placed in an airtight storage bag

PLACE IN THE FREEZER:

* The lamb tagine, if you are serving it more than 2 days after preparing it
* The velouté soup, in the large jar, leaving a little air at the top
* The leek and potato gratin, in its baking dish, covered with plastic wrap
* The lamb keftas with the cooked turnip-carrot-chickpea mixture, in a large airtight container
* The salmon and spinach lasagna, directly in the baking dish covered with plastic wrap

EACH NIGHT'S PREP

MONDAY

Appetizer: Tuna rillettes endive bites

Main: Turnip, honey, and goat cheese tart Tatin

Reheating time: 10 minutes

Preparation time: 2 minutes

Ingredients: the tuna rillettes, the Belgian endive, the tart Tatin

Pull off the individual leaves of the Belgian endive, wash, dry with paper towels, and fill each one with a little of the tuna rillettes.

Reheat the tart Tatin in the oven preheated to 325°F (160°C).

For Tuesday, if you have frozen the lamb tagine, remove it from the freezer and thaw it in the refrigerator.

TUESDAY

Main: Lamb tagine with quince

Reheating time: 15 minutes

Cooking time: 5 minutes

Preparation time: 1 minute

Ingredients: the lamb tagine, the couscous, half the remaining cilantro

Reheat the lamb tagine in its pot. Cook the couscous according to the package directions.

Serve the couscous on plates, topped with the lamb tagine, and sprinkled with chopped cilantro.

For Wednesday, remove the velouté soup and the potato and leek gratin from the freezer and thaw them in the refrigerator.

WEDNESDAY

Appetizer: Spinach and *fromage frais* velouté soup

Main: Potato, leek, onion, and lardons gratin

Reheating time: 15 minutes

Ingredients: the potato and leek gratin, the velouté soup

Reheat the gratin in the oven preheated to 325°F (160°C).

Reheat the velouté soup in a saucepan and serve.

For Thursday, remove the lamb keftas and the turnip-carrot-chickpea mixture from the freezer and thaw them in the refrigerator.

THURSDAY

Main: Lamb keftas, panfried carrots, turnips, and chickpeas with cumin

Reheating time: 15 minutes

Ingredients: the keftas, panfried carrots, turnips, and chickpeas with cumin, the remaining cilantro

Reheat the keftas in a sauté pan. Sprinkle them with chopped cilantro.

For Friday, remove the salmon and spinach lasagna from the freezer and thaw it in the refrigerator.

FRIDAY

Main: Salmon and spinach lasagna

Reheating time: 15 minutes

Ingredients: the salmon and spinach lasagna

Reheat the lasagna in the oven preheated to 325°F (160°C) and serve.

MENU #4

SHOPPING LIST MENU #4

FRUITS / VEGETABLES

* 1 (4½-lb/2-kg) fresh pumpkin
* 1¾ lb (800 g) small potatoes
* 1 broccoli crown
* 2 carrots
* 1 small container cherry tomatoes (about 6 oz/170 g)
* 1 celery stalk
* 1 bunch cilantro
* 6 garlic cloves
* 6 yellow onions
* 6 shallots

PANTRY AND STAPLES

* 9 oz (250 g) dried pasta shells (long tube)
* 1⅓ cups (9 oz/250 g) microwaveable pouch of quick-cooking white or light brown rice
* 1 cup (7 oz/200 g) couscous
* Ground cinnamon
* Ground cumin
* Ground turmeric
* Ground ginger
* Curry powder
* Dried thyme
* All-purpose flour

* Wine vinegar
* Olive oil
* Salt, black pepper

MEAT / FISH

* 3 skin-on chicken thighs
* 4 prepackaged frozen pollack fillets (or other similar white-flesh fish)
* 4 slices ham (or sliced cooked turkey breast)

COLD CASE

* ¾ cup (3½ oz/100 g) grated Parmesan cheese
* 1⅔ cups (13⅓ oz/377 g) crème fraîche
* 1¼ to 1¾ cups (2½ to 3½ oz/70 to 100 g) shredded Gruyère cheese
* 9 tbsp (4½ oz/125 g) unsalted butter
* 1⅓ cups (320 mL) heavy cream
* 1 prepared puff pastry sheet (about 8 oz/227 g)

DRY AND CANNED GOODS

* 1 can red kidney beans (about 14 oz/400 g), drained
* 1⅔ cups (400 mL) peeled tomatoes, in their juice
* 1 handful dried pumpkin seeds

MENUS

MONDAY

Appetizer: Cherry tomatoes, Parmesan, squash seeds, and thyme in flaky pastry

Main: Vegetarian chili

TUESDAY

Pumpkin and chicken couscous

WEDNESDAY

Ham* and broccoli noodle bake

THURSDAY

Chicken and vegetable crumble

FRIDAY

Appetizer: Pumpkin curry velouté soup

Main: Pollack in shallot sauce, steamed potatoes

For a pork-free menu, replace the ham with turkey breast.

SET UP

If you have enough work space, set out all the ingredients needed for this cooking session. This includes everything except the potatoes, pollack, puff pastry sheet, rice, and couscous. This allows you to have everything at your fingertips and to not lose time searching for the ingredients in the pantry or refrigerator.

SET OUT THE NECESSARY EQUIPMENT:

* 1 baking sheet
* 2 gratin baking dishes (or shallow baking dishes)
* 1 large sauté pan
* 1 large saucepan
* 1 small saucepan
* 1 lidded Dutch oven or stockpot
* 1 immersion blender
* 1 skimmer
* 1 large mixing bowl
* 1 small mixing bowl

* 3 small bowls
* 1 (6-cup/1.5-L-capacity) glass jar (for storing the velouté soup)
* 1 salad spinner (or large bowl and clean kitchen towel)
* 2 containers: 1 large + 1 small
* Paper towels, aluminum foil, plastic wrap, parchment

EVERYTHING IS NOW READY FOR A COOKING TIME OF 1 HOUR AND 50 MINUTES!

1. In the large sauté pan, heat 2 tbsp (30 mL) of olive oil until warm. Add the chicken thighs skin side down. Cover, and cook for 10 minutes, or until lightly browned.

2. Peel and roughly chop the onions, shallots, and garlic cloves. Place them separately in the small bowls.

3. Fill the salad spinner (or a large bowl) with water and soak the cilantro for 5 minutes. Drain, then gently spin the cilantro dry (or use the kitchen towel). Place the cilantro in a glass container between two sheets of paper towels. Refrigerate for up to 1 week.

4. Turn off the heat under the chicken. Peel the carrots, and wash the celery stalk. Cut the carrots and celery into small dice. Turn the chicken thighs over (be careful of spattering), add one-fourth of the onions, one-fourth of the garlic, and all of the carrots and celery. Season with salt, add ½ tsp of cinnamon, and ½ tsp of ground ginger. Turn on the heat under the chicken to low. Add about ¾ cup (180 mL) of water, cover, and let cook for 35 minutes.

5. Prepare the vegetarian chili: In the Dutch oven, heat 2 tbsp (30 mL) of olive oil until warm, then add one-third of the remaining onions and garlic, and 1 tsp of salt. Let cook for 10 minutes, covered, over low heat.

6. Meanwhile, cut the pumpkin in half, scrape out and discard the seeds, then peel the flesh and cut it into large cubes. Add 1 handful of the cubes to a gratin dish that will be used with the crumble topping. Place the remaining cubes in the large mixing bowl.

7. To the Dutch oven, add the peeled tomatoes with their juice, ½ tsp of turmeric, and ½ tsp of cumin. Continue cooking for another 15 minutes.

8. Fill the large saucepan with salted water and bring it to a boil. Meanwhile, wash the broccoli and cut it into very small florets. Add the florets to the saucepan, stir to incorporate, then let cook for 10 minutes.

9. Preheat the oven to 350°F (180°C). Prepare the crumble topping in the small mixing bowl by combining 1½ cups (5¼ oz/150 g) of flour, the butter, ½ cup (2 oz/60 g) of Parmesan, 1 pinch of thyme, and half the dried pumpkin seeds. Set aside.

10. Remove the cooked broccoli florets from the saucepan using the skimmer, and transfer them to a bowl. Add the pasta shells to the pot. Cook just until the pasta is al dente (still firm to the bite).

11. Drain and rinse the beans and add them to the pot. Stir to combine, and turn off the heat.

12. Remove 1 chicken thigh from the sauté pan and set it aside on a plate to cool. Cut the cherry tomatoes in half. Place half of them in the gratin dish with the pumpkin cubes. Add one-third of the broccoli florets, half the remaining onions and garlic, and a little salt. Shred the flesh of the chicken thigh that is cooling on the plate. Add the shredded meat to the gratin dish, and stir to combine. Cover the mixture with the crumble topping. Bake for 30 minutes, or until golden on top.

13. To the small saucepan, add a scant ¼ cup (50 mL) of vinegar and all of the shallots. Let cook over low heat for about 15 minutes, just until almost all of the vinegar has evaporated.

14. Drain the pasta and place it in the separate gratin dish. Add the remaining broccoli, the cream, and half the remaining garlic to the dish. Dice the ham, add it to the gratin dish, season with salt and pepper, and stir to thoroughly combine. Sprinkle the shredded Gruyère over the top, and bake for 15 minutes, or until the cheese is melted and golden. Wash the large saucepan, fill it half full with water, and bring it to a boil.

15. To the sauté pan with the chicken thighs, add one-third of the pumpkin cubes. Continue cooking for 10 more minutes, or until the chicken is cooked through and the vegetables are softened.

16. To the saucepan of boiling water, add the remaining pumpkin cubes, garlic, and onions. Let cook for 15 minutes.

17. To the small saucepan with the shallots, add two-thirds of crème fraîche (about 9 oz/250 g), and season with salt and pepper. Set aside off the heat.

18. Remove the puff pastry sheet from the refrigerator, roll it out, and cut it into twelve 4-in. (10-cm)

PLACE IN THE REFRIGERATOR:

* The puff pastry squares, directly on the baking sheet, covered in foil (keeps for 2 days)
* The vegetarian chili, in the pot (keeps for 3 days)
* The pumpkin and chicken (keeps for 2 days)
* The cilantro, in its airtight container (keeps for 1 week)

PLACE IN THE FREEZER:

* The pumpkin and chicken, if you are serving it more than 2 days after preparing it
* The velouté soup, in the large jar, leaving a little room at the top
* The ham and broccoli noodle bake, in its gratin dish, covered with plastic wrap
* The chicken and vegetable crumble, in its gratin dish, covered with plastic wrap
* The shallot sauce, in an airtight container

squares. Place 3 cherry tomato halves in the center of each puff pastry square, and gather the ends to the center and pinch them together to seal the dough. Sprinkle the squares with the remaining Parmesan, some thyme, and some pumpkin seeds. Place the squares on the baking sheet lined with parchment paper, and bake for 10 minutes, or until puffed and golden.

19. To the large saucepan with the pumpkin, add the remaining crème fraîche and ½ tsp of curry powder. Blend thoroughly with the immersion blender.

EACH NIGHT'S PREP

MONDAY

Appetizer: Cherry tomatoes, Parmesan, squash seeds, and thyme in flaky pastry

Main: Vegetarian chili

Reheating time: 10 minutes

Cooking time: 10 minutes

Preparation time: 1 minute

Ingredients: the rice, the puff pastry squares, the vegetarian chili, half the cilantro

Cook the rice according to the package directions. Reheat the puff pastry squares in the oven preheated to 325°F (160°C). Reheat the chili in its pot. Serve with the rice, sprinkled with cilantro.

For Tuesday, if you have frozen the pumpkin and chicken, remove it from the freezer and thaw it in the refrigerator.

TUESDAY

Main: Pumpkin and chicken couscous

Reheating time: 15 minutes

Cooking time: 5 minutes

Preparation time: 1 minute

Ingredients: the pumpkin and chicken, the couscous, the remaining cilantro

Reheat the pumpkin and chicken in a sauté pan. Cook the couscous according to the package directions. Serve the couscous on plates, with the pumpkin and chicken ladled over the top, and sprinkled with chopped cilantro.

For Wednesday, remove the ham and broccoli noodle bake from the freezer and thaw it in the refrigerator.

WEDNESDAY

Main: Ham and broccoli noodle bake

Reheating time: 15 minutes

Ingredients: the ham and broccoli noodle bake

Reheat the noodle bake in the oven preheated to 325°F (160°C) and serve.

For Thursday, remove the chicken and vegetable crumble from the freezer and thaw it in the refrigerator.

MENU #4

THURSDAY

Main: Chicken and vegetable crumble

Reheating time: 15 minutes

Ingredients: the chicken and vegetable crumble

Reheat the crumble in the oven preheated to 325°F (160°C) and serve.

For Friday, remove the pumpkin curry velouté soup and the shallot sauce from the freezer and thaw them in the refrigerator.

FRIDAY

Appetizer: Pumpkin curry velouté soup

Main: Pollack in shallot sauce, steamed potatoes

Reheating time: 15 minutes

Cooking time: 15 minutes

Preparation time: 2 minutes

Ingredients: the potatoes, the frozen pollack fillets, the velouté soup, the shallot sauce

Wash and steam the whole potatoes, skin on, for 15 minutes, or until tender when pierced with a fork. Cook the fillets according to the package directions (or according to your preference). Meanwhile, reheat the soup in a large saucepan, and the shallot sauce in a small saucepan. Serve the pollack and the potatoes with the sauce spooned over the top.

WINTER

MENU #1

SHOPPING CART MENU #1

SHOPPING LIST   MENU #1

FRUITS / VEGETABLES

* 6 leeks
* 8 carrots
* 1 celery stalk
* 4 turnips
* 2¼ lb (2 kg) Charlotte potatoes (or similar waxy salad potato)
* 1 bunch flat-leaf parsley
* 2 white or yellow onions
* 1 garlic clove

PANTRY AND STAPLES

* 7 oz (200 g) orzo pasta (or broken vermicelli)
* 3 bay leaves
* Dried thyme
* Mustard
* Vinegar
* Sunflower oil
* Olive oil
* Salt, fleur de sel sea salt, coarse gray sea salt, black pepper

MEAT / FISH

* 3⅓ lb (1.5 kg) beef stewing meat (a mixture of top and lower beef rib meat, upper chuck, and shank)
* 1 to 4 marrowbones, according to your tastes
* 14 oz (400 g) smoked haddock fillets

COLD CASE

* 6 large eggs
* 1⅔ cups (400 mL) heavy cream

DRY AND CANNED GOODS

* Just over ¾ cup (200 mL) coconut milk
* 1 small jar cornichons (gherkins), about 7 oz/200 g
* 4 slices rustic bread
* 1 package feuilles de brick (or phyllo dough)
* 3 large peppercorns
* 3 whole cloves

MENUS

MONDAY
Appetizer: Leeks in vinaigrette with deviled eggs

Main: Orzo pasta in beef broth

TUESDAY
Pot-au-feu

WEDNESDAY
Appetizer: Beef and vegetable samosas

Main: Haddock brandade

THURSDAY
Vegetable velouté soup, marrow toasts

FRIDAY
Haddock and coconut milk soup

SET UP

If you have enough work space, set out all the ingredients needed for this cooking session. This includes everything except 1 egg, the pasta, cornichons, mustard, sunflower oil, and fleur de sel sea salt. This allows you to have everything at your fingertips and to not lose time searching for the ingredients in the pantry or refrigerator.

SET OUT THE NECESSARY EQUIPMENT:

* 1 small saucepan
* 1 medium saucepan
* 1 very large saucepan
* 1 large lidded Dutch oven or 1 stockpot (for making the pot-au-feu)
* 2 large mixing bowls
* 1 gratin baking dish (or shallow baking dish)
* 1 food mill (or potato masher)
* 1 immersion blender
* 1 skimmer
* 1 colander
* 2 (6-cup/1.5-L-capacity) glass jars (for storing the pot-au-feu broth and the velouté)
* 6 containers: 3 large + 2 medium + 1 small
* Plastic wrap

EVERYTHING IS NOW READY FOR A COOKING TIME OF 2 HOURS!

1. Place the pieces of beef (but not the marrow-bones) in the Dutch oven. Add 3 quarts (2.9 L) of water, 1 tbsp of coarse gray sea salt, 2 bay leaves, and 1 onion that has been peeled and studded with the cloves. Bring to a boil. Let cook, uncovered, for 15 minutes, skimming the fat from the surface during that time, then lower the heat.

2. Meanwhile, in the medium saucepan, heat the coconut milk with 2 cups (480 mL) of water, 1 bay leaf, and ½ tsp of dried thyme.

3. Thoroughly rinse the haddock fillets under cold water to remove excess salt. Remove the skin

using your fingers. Cut the fillets into pieces, then place them in the saucepan in the coconut milk. Let cook over very low heat for 15 minutes without boiling.

4. Fill the very large saucepan with salted water and bring it to a boil. Peel all the potatoes. Cook the potatoes whole in the saucepan just until tender when pierced with a fork (about 30 minutes).

5. Remove the pieces of haddock from the saucepan using the skimmer, and place them in the colander set over a plate to drain (do not drain the saucepan).

6. Peel the turnips, carrots, and the remaining onion. Dice 1 turnip, and cut the remaining turnips in half. Cut 2 of the carrots into rounds, and cut the remaining carrots into quarters. Dice the onion.

7. To the saucepan used to poach the haddock, add the diced turnips and onions and the carrot rounds. Let cook for 30 minutes, covered; do not add salt during this time.

8. To the pot with the beef, add the turnip halves, carrot pieces, peppercorns, and 1 sprig of parsley.

9. Cut off the root ends of the leeks, thoroughly wash the leeks (including in between the leaves), and cut them each into four sections. Pick the leaves off the celery stalk, wash the stalk, and cut it into four equal pieces. Add the celery and leeks to the pot with the beef.

10. In the large mixing bowl, crumble half the pieces of haddock. Peel and chop the garlic clove and add it to the bowl, then add just over ¾ cup (200 mL) of the cream, 2 tbsp (30 mL) of olive oil, and two-thirds of the cooked potatoes. Season with pepper but do not add salt. Process the mixture using the food mill (or potato masher).

11. Wash and dry the parsley, then finely chop it. Add half the chopped parsley to the haddock mixture. Stir to combine, then transfer it to the gratin dish. Wash out the bowl.

12. Place the remaining haddock fillets in the saucepan with the vegetables and coconut milk. Turn off the heat and let cool.

13. Add water to the small saucepan and bring it to a boil. Cook 4 of the eggs in the boiling water for 10 minutes.

14. Remove all of the vegetables from the pot with the beef using the skimmer. Set aside 8 attractive sections of the leeks in a small container to serve with the leek vinaigrette. Sprinkle them with 1 tbsp of chopped parsley. Set aside the most attractive pieces of carrots, turnips, leeks, celery, and onion to serve on the side with the pot-au-feu.

15. Remove half the meat from the ribs and shred it. Combine the shredded meat with 3 of the potatoes, 2 pieces of turnips, several carrot rounds, the remaining chopped parsley, and salt and pepper. Place the mixture in a bowl to make the stuffing for the samosas.

16. Place the broken pieces of vegetables in the large mixing bowl to make the velouté soup. Add

1 potato, the remaining cream, 2 ladles of pot-au-feu broth from the pot, and a little salt and pepper. Blend thoroughly using the immersion blender. Store in a glass jar.

17. Add the marrowbones to the pot, then continue cooking for as long as time permits (ideally another 1 hour and 30 minutes).

18. Preheat the oven to 350°F (180°C). Cut each sheet of feuilles de brick in half. Fold over the rounded sides in toward the center. Spoon 1 tsp of the samosa stuffing onto the pointed end closest to you. Fold the sheets starting from the end with the stuffing, alternating from left to right and moving toward the top to form a triangle. Tuck any excess portion of the dough inside to close up the triangle. (Although this technique is not complicated, it does take some time to complete. If you need some little hands to help you with this step, kids are always delighted to assist.) Lightly beat 1 egg, and brush the samosas with it. Bake for 15 minutes, or until golden and crisp.

IT'S ALL DONE! LET COOL.

PLACE IN THE REFRIGERATOR:

* The 4 hard-boiled eggs (keeps for 5 days)
* The 8 sections of cooked leeks (keeps for 3 days)
* The pot-au-feu broth, in the glass jar (keeps for 3 days)
* The pot-au-feu stewing meat, if you are serving it within 2 days of preparing it
* The pot-au-feu vegetables (keeps for 3 days)

PLACE IN THE FREEZER:

* The pot-au-feu stewing meat, if you are serving it more than 2 days after preparing it
* The samosas
* The haddock brandade, in its gratin dish, covered with plastic wrap
* The velouté soup
* The marrowbones with a little broth
* The slices of rustic bread, in an airtight container
* The haddock and coconut milk soup

EACH NIGHT'S PREP

MONDAY

Appetizer: Leeks in vinaigrette with deviled eggs

Main: Orzo pasta in beef broth

Cooking time: 10 minutes

Preparation time: 20 minutes

Ingredients: mustard, vinegar, olive oil, the 8 sections of cooked leeks, the remaining uncooked egg, sunflower oil, the 4 hard-boiled eggs, the pot-au-feu broth, the orzo pasta, salt, and pepper

Prepare the vinaigrette: Combine 1 tsp (5 g) of mustard with 1 tsp (5 g) of vinegar and a little salt and pepper. Whisk vigorously while drizzling in 2 tbsp (30 mL) of olive oil a little at a time. Pour the vinaigrette over the leeks.

Prepare the filling for the deviled eggs: Combine the 1 raw egg yolk with 1 tsp (5 g) of mustard and a little salt and pepper. Whisk vigorously while adding 4 tbsp (60 mL) of sunflower oil a little at a time. Peel the hard-boiled eggs. Cut them in half. Remove the yolks, and incorporate them into the mixture. Fill the empty egg white halves with this mixture. Serve with the leeks. Remove and discard the layer of fat from the broth. Cook the pasta in the broth. Serve.

For Tuesday, if you have frozen the pot-au-feu stewing meat, remove it from the freezer and thaw in the refrigerator.

TUESDAY

Main: Pot-au-feu

Reheating time: 10 minutes

Ingredients: the pot-au-feu vegetables, the pot-au-feu stewing meat, cornichons, mustard, fleur de sel sea salt

Reheat the vegetables and meat. Serve each person one piece of each kind of meat served with the cornichons, mustard, and fleur de sel sea salt.

For Wednesday, remove the samosas and the haddock brandade from the freezer and thaw them in the refrigerator.

WEDNESDAY

Appetizer: Beef and vegetable samosas

Main: Haddock brandade

Reheating time: 10 minutes

Ingredients: the samosas, the haddock brandade

Preheat the oven to 350°F (180°C), and reheat the samosas and the brandade for 10 minutes.

For Thursday, remove the vegetable velouté soup, the marrowbones, and the bread slices from the freezer and thaw them in the refrigerator.

THURSDAY

Main: Vegetable velouté soup, marrow toasts

Reheating time: 15 minutes

Preparation time: 2 minutes

Ingredients: the vegetable velouté soup, the marrowbones, the slices of bread, fleur de sel sea salt

Reheat the velouté soup in a saucepan. Reheat the marrowbones with the broth in a small saucepan. Toast the slices of bread. Spread the marrow on the bread, and sprinkle with fleur de sel sea salt.

For Friday, remove the haddock and coconut milk soup from the freezer and thaw it in the refrigerator.

FRIDAY

Main: Haddock and coconut milk soup

Reheating time: 15 minutes

Ingredients: the haddock and coconut milk soup

Reheat the soup in a saucepan, and serve.

MENU #2

SHOPPING CART MENU #2

SHOPPING LIST MENU #2

FRUITS / VEGETABLES

* 18 oz (500 g) white button mushrooms
* 2 leeks
* 4 carrots
* ½ head red cabbage (or 1 bag of grated red cabbage, about 9 oz/250 g, sell-by date > 3 or 4 days)
* 2¼ lb (1 kg) Charlotte potatoes (or similar waxy salad potato)
* 1 bag (about 9 oz/250 g) field greens, sell-by date > 2 days
* 1 small bunch red grapes
* 1 Pink Lady or Red Delicious apple
* 2 shallots
* 2 yellow onions
* 4 garlic cloves
* 1 small knob (half the size of your thumb) fresh ginger, grated (optional)

PANTRY AND STAPLES

* 2½ cups (18 oz/500 g) quick-cooking lentils
* 1⅓ cups (9 oz/250 g) microwaveable pouch of quick-cooking white rice
* Mustard
* Soy sauce
* Honey

* Ketchup
* Cornstarch
* Dried thyme
* Whole nutmeg
* Wine vinegar
* Olive oil
* Salt, black pepper

MEAT / FISH

* 5¼ oz (150 g) smoked lardons or diced turkey
* 2¼ lb (1 kg) veal stew meat
* 16 chicken wings
* 1 chorizo sausage

COLD CASE

* 4 large eggs
* 1⅔ cups (400 mL) heavy cream
* 2 cups (16 oz/454 g) crème fraîche
* 1 small container shredded Gruyère cheese (about 4 oz/113 g)
* 1 (9-in./23-cm) piecrust

DRY AND CANNED GOODS

* 1¾ oz (50 g) pitted black olives
* Scant ½ cup (100 mL) port or red wine
* 1 large can tomato paste (about 12 oz/350 g)

MENUS

MONDAY
Quiche lorraine*

TUESDAY
Appetizer: Leek and potato velouté soup

Main: Caramelized chicken wings

WEDNESDAY
Appetizer: Red cabbage, grape, and apple salad

Main: Slow-cooked veal and chorizo* stew

THURSDAY
Cream of lentils, mushrooms, and carrots

FRIDAY
Spicy veal blanquette

For a pork-free menu, replace the lardons in the quiche with diced turkey meat, and the chorizo with a pinch of ground chile pepper.

SET UP

If you have enough work space, set out all the ingredients needed for this cooking session. This includes everything except the red cabbage (if using a bag of grated), the bag of field greens, the grapes, apple, lentils, and rice. This allows you to have everything at your fingertips and to not lose time searching for the ingredients in the pantry or refrigerator.

SET OUT THE NECESSARY EQUIPMENT:

* 1 lidded Dutch oven or stockpot
* 1 (8-in./20-cm) tart pan
* Ceramic pie weights (or dried beans)
* 1 small saucepan
* 1 medium saucepan
* 1 large mixing bowl
* 1 skillet
* 1 immersion blender
* 1 small grater or zester (for the nutmeg)

* 5 containers: 3 large + 1 medium + 1 small for the vinaigrette
* Paper towels, parchment paper

EVERYTHING IS NOW READY FOR A COOKING TIME OF 1 HOUR AND 45 MINUTES!

1. Peel and thinly slice the onions and garlic cloves. Cut the veal into cubes. In the Dutch oven, heat 1 tbsp (15 mL) of olive oil until warm, then add half the onions and garlic, the veal cubes, 1 tsp of salt, and a little pepper. Let cook for 10 minutes.

2. Meanwhile, peel all of the potatoes and carrots. Cut the potatoes into large dice and cut the carrots into rounds.

3. To the pot, add ½ tsp of thyme and all of the tomato paste. Stir to thoroughly combine. Add the port, then add just enough water to cover the meat. Add three-fourths of the diced potatoes, one-third of the carrot rounds, and the chorizo,

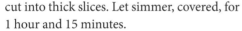

cut into thick slices. Let simmer, covered, for 1 hour and 15 minutes.

4. Preheat the oven to 375°F (190°C). Grease the tart pan. Line the pan with the piecrust, gently pressing the dough down into the pan and up the sides. Trim off any excess dough from around the edges, level with the top of the pan. Prick the bottom of the crust all over with a fork. Crumple the parchment paper included in the package with the piecrust (or use parchment paper), place it on top of the piecrust in the pan, then fill the pan with the pie weights. Prebake the crust for 25 minutes, or until pale golden.

5. Bring a medium saucepan filled with 3⅓ cups (800 mL) of salted water to a boil. Cut off the root ends of the leeks and any rough ends of the green portion, then thoroughly wash the leeks (including in between the leaves). Cut the white portion of the leeks into thick rounds, then dice the green portion. In the saucepan, combine the white portion of the leeks, the remaining potatoes, and

the remaining onions. Reduce to a simmer and let cook for 25 minutes.

6. Fill the small saucepan with salted water and bring it to a boil. Cook the remaining carrot rounds for 20 minutes, or until softened.

7. Prepare the vinaigrette: In the small container, add 2 tbsp (30 g) of mustard, ½ tsp of salt, and 1 pinch of pepper. Add 4 tbsp (60 mL) of vinegar, and stir to combine. Slowly add 8 tbsp (120 mL) of olive oil while whisking vigorously.

8. Prepare the quiche filling: In the mixing bowl, beat together the eggs with ½ tsp of salt, a little pepper, and some freshly grated nutmeg. Whisk in the cream.

9. In the skillet without any added fat, brown the lardons for 5 minutes over high heat. Dab any excess fat from the skillet using a paper towel. Add the cooked lardons to the bottom of the prebaked crust, distribute the Gruyère over the top, and pour in the filling. Bake for 30 minutes, or until golden on top.

10. To the saucepan with the leeks and potatoes, add 2 tbsp (1 oz/30 g) of the crème fraîche, and thoroughly blend using the immersion blender.

11. Peel and thinly slice the shallots. In the skillet, heat 1 tbsp (15 mL) of olive oil until warm. Add the shallots, the remaining garlic, and ½ tsp of salt. Let cook gently for 5 minutes, then add the diced leek greens. Briefly wash the mushrooms and thinly slice them. Add them to the skillet. Let cook for 5 minutes.

12. Cut half of the cooked carrot rounds into small dice. Place them in the medium-size container.

13. Add the remaining crème fraîche to the skillet, then add 1 tbsp (⅓ oz/10 g) of cornstarch. Cook for 5 minutes, or until slightly thickened. Add one-third of this mixture to the container with the diced carrots; this will serve as the cream for the lentils on Thursday.

14. In the skillet, place the cooked carrot rounds. Remove half the pieces of veal from the pot and place them in the skillet. Stir well to combine.

15. Add the olives to the pot, and continue cooking for 10 minutes.

16. Prepare the marinade for the chicken wings: In a large container, add 6 tbsp (90 mL) of soy sauce, 4 tbsp (80 g) of honey, 2 tbsp (30 g) of ketchup, and the fresh ginger (grated, if using). Stir to combine, then immerse the chicken wings in the marinade.

17. If the red cabbage is whole, grate it and place it in an airtight container.

IT'S ALL DONE! LET COOL.

PLACE IN THE REFRIGERATOR:

* The quiche lorraine, in its pan (keeps for 2 days)
* The velouté soup, in its pot (keeps for 3 days)
* The chicken wings, in their marinade (keeps for 3 days)
* The vinaigrette (keeps for 1 week)

PLACE IN THE FREEZER:

* The veal and chorizo stew
* The creamed vegetables for the lentils
* The veal blanquette

EACH NIGHT'S PREP

MONDAY

Main: Quiche lorraine

Reheating time: 10 minutes

Ingredients: the quiche lorraine, the bag of field greens, half the vinaigrette

Reheat the quiche for 10 minutes in the oven preheated to 350°F (180°C). Serve with the field greens and the vinaigrette on the side.

TUESDAY

Appetizer: Leek and potato velouté soup

Main: Caramelized chicken wings

Reheating time: 10 minutes

Cooking time: 40 minutes

Ingredients: the marinated chicken wings, the leek and potato velouté soup, black pepper

Preheat the oven to 475°F (250°C). Place the chicken wings with their marinade in a baking dish, and bake for about 40 minutes, just until they are well caramelized.

Reheat the velouté soup for 10 minutes over low heat, season with a little pepper, and serve.

For Wednesday, remove the veal and chorizo stew from the freezer and thaw it in the refrigerator.

WEDNESDAY

Appetizer: Red cabbage, grape, and apple salad

Main: Slow-cooked veal and chorizo stew

Reheating time: 15 minutes

Preparation time: 10 minutes

Ingredients: the thawed veal and chorizo stew, the apple, the grapes, the red cabbage, the remaining vinaigrette

Reheat the stew for 15 minutes over low heat. Slice the apple into thin wedges. Cut the grapes in half and remove any seeds. Add the grated cabbage, apple slices, and grapes to a large bowl. Add the vinaigrette, stir to combine, and serve.

For Thursday, remove the container with the creamed vegetables from the freezer and thaw it in the refrigerator.

MENU #2

THURSDAY

Main: Cream of lentils, mushrooms, and carrots

Reheating time: 10 minutes

Ingredients: the package of lentils, the creamed vegetables

Top the lentils with the creamed vegetables. Reheat the dish in either a saucepan or the microwave for a few minutes as needed, according to your preference.

For Friday, remove the veal blanquette from the freezer and thaw it in the refrigerator.

FRIDAY

Main: Spicy veal blanquette

Reheating time: 15 minutes

Cooking time: 10 minutes

Ingredients: the rice, the veal blanquette

Cook the rice according to the package directions. Reheat the veal blanquette according to your preference, in either a saucepan or the microwave for a few minutes as needed. Serve with the rice.

MENU #3

SHOPPING LIST   MENU #3

FRUITS / VEGETABLES

* 1 small celery root
* 1 parsnip
* 1 large broccoli crown
* 3 organic oranges
* 3 blood oranges
* 2¼ lb (1 kg) Charlotte potatoes (or similar waxy salad potato)
* 1 small red kuri squash (potimarron)
* 1 carrot
* 1 handful bean sprouts
* 1 bunch parsley
* 1 yellow onion
* 1 (2-in./5-cm) knob fresh ginger
* 1 shallot
* 7 garlic cloves

PANTRY AND STAPLES

* 1¼ cups (7 oz/200 g) quinoa
* 9 oz (250 g) spaghetti noodles
* Honey
* Dried thyme
* Soy sauce
* Olive oil
* Whole nutmeg

* Quatre épices spice blend
* Cornstarch
* Curry powder
* Ground cumin
* Salt, black pepper

MEAT / FISH

* 4 small duck (or duckling) breasts
* 1 (16-oz/454-g) package frozen small (bay) scallops

COLD CASE

* 4 large eggs
* 3⅓ cups (800 mL) heavy cream
* 1 cup (8 oz/227 g) crème fraîche
* 4 cups (960 mL) low-fat milk
* 1 small round fresh goat cheese (about 2 oz/60 g)

DRY AND CANNED GOODS

* 1 package dried Chinese wheat noodles (about 8 oz/227 g)
* 1 (15-oz/425-g) can chickpeas
* 6 tbsp (2 oz/60 g) raw or toasted unsalted hazelnuts
* Scant ½ cup (100 mL) white wine

MENUS

MONDAY

Appetizer: Celery root and parsnip velouté soup with scallops

Main: Crustless goat cheese and broccoli quiche

TUESDAY

Duck breast à l'orange, scalloped potatoes

WEDNESDAY

Appetizer: Chickpea and orange salad

Main: Roasted red kuri squash, quinoa, goat cheese, hazelnuts

THURSDAY

Duck and noodles Chinese stir-fry

FRIDAY

Scallop spaghetti

SET UP

If you have enough work space, set out all the ingredients needed for this cooking session. This includes everything except the bean sprouts, duck breasts, scallops, crème fraîche, wheat noodles, chickpeas, spaghetti noodles, cumin, quatre épices spice blend, and white wine. This allows you to have everything at your fingertips and to not lose time searching for the ingredients in the pantry or refrigerator.

SET OUT THE NECESSARY EQUIPMENT:

* 1 medium saucepan
* 1 large saucepan
* 1 mixing bowl
* 1 food processor or mandoline slicer
* 1 small grater or zester (for the orange zest and nutmeg)
* 2 gratin baking dishes (or shallow baking dishes)
* 1 fine-mesh strainer
* 1 (8-in./20-cm) round cake pan
* 1 immersion blender

* 1 salad spinner (or clean kitchen towel)
* 1 small bowl
* 8 containers: 1 large + 2 medium + 5 small
* 2 small lidded glass jars (for the toasted hazelnuts and the garlic and shallots)
* Paper towels

EVERYTHING IS NOW READY FOR A COOKING TIME OF 2 HOURS!

1. Preheat the oven to 325°F (160°C). Peel the potatoes. Very thinly slice them using the food processor or mandoline; do not rinse them. Peel 4 of the garlic cloves, finely chop them, and set them aside in a small bowl.

2. Arrange half the potato slices in a gratin dish. Season with salt, grate a little fresh nutmeg on top, then top with ½ tsp of chopped garlic. Arrange the remaining potato slices on top, and season with salt and a little freshly grated nutmeg. Pour just over ¾ cup (200 mL) of the cream and 2 cups

(480 mL) of the milk over the top of the potatoes. Bake on a rack set near the bottom of the oven for 1 hour and 30 minutes, or until golden on top and bubbling.

3. In the medium saucepan, bring salted water to a boil. Cut the broccoli into florets. Place two-thirds of the florets into the boiling water. Let cook for 10 minutes. Set aside the remaining florets in a medium-size container.

4. Prepare the quiche filling: In the mixing bowl, lightly beat the eggs. Add 1⅔ cups (400 mL) of the cream, ½ tsp of garlic, and 1 tbsp (⅓ oz/10 g) of cornstarch. Season with salt and pepper. Dice half the goat cheese. Drain the parboiled broccoli florets and distribute them and the diced goat cheese on the bottom of the cake pan. Pour the quiche filling over the top. Bake for 40 minutes, or until golden, on a rack placed near the top of the oven.

5. To the large saucepan, add the remaining 2 cups (480 mL) of milk, and just over ¾ cup (200 mL) of water. Season with salt and bring to a simmer. Peel

the celery root and parsnip. Cut them into large dice. Place them in the saucepan, and let cook for 20 minutes, or until softened.

6. Wash, dry, and zest the organic oranges; set the zest aside. Peel the oranges and cut out each section with a knife, cutting between the white membrane. Press the empty membranes of the oranges over an airtight container to release their juice; reserve. Place the orange sections and zest in the juice.

7. Repeat these steps with the blood oranges (minus the zest), and place the juice and sections in a separate small airtight container.

8. In the medium saucepan, bring salted water to a boil. Thoroughly rinse the quinoa in the fine-mesh strainer. Cook the quinoa for 15 minutes, or just until tender, in the boiling water, then drain.

9. Wash the red kuri squash. Using a large knife, cut the squash in half and peel (reserve the skin; it can be eaten). Scrape out the seeds. Slice the flesh, then dice it. Place the flesh in the separate gratin

dish with the 3 whole garlic cloves, 1 tbsp (10 g) of thyme, 3 tbsp (45 mL) of olive oil, and some salt and pepper. After the gratin has finished cooking, increase the oven temperature to 400°F (200°C) and place the baking dish with the squash on a rack near the top of the oven. Bake for 30 minutes, or until tender when pierced with a fork.

10. Peel the carrot and cut it into julienne (thin matchstick strips). Place the strips into a container with the raw broccoli florets.

11. Peel and thinly slice the shallot. Place the slices in a small jar with half the remaining chopped garlic, and seal the jar so that it's airtight.

12. Peel and thinly slice the onion and ginger. Place them in an airtight container with the remaining chopped garlic.

13. In an airtight container, combine 4 tbsp (60 mL) of soy sauce with 4 tbsp (80 g) of honey.

14. Using the immersion blender, blend the celery root and parsnip with the remaining cream and ½ tsp of curry powder.

15. Wash the parsley, place in the salad spinner, and spin to dry (or gently dry with the kitchen towel). Place it in a large container between two sheets of paper towels.

16. If the hazelnuts are not toasted, toast them in the oven for 5 minutes. Roughly chop them, and place them in the jar.

IT'S ALL DONE! LET COOL.

PLACE IN THE REFRIGERATOR:

* The cooked quinoa (keeps for 3 to 4 days)
* The velouté soup, in the saucepan (keeps for 3 days)
* The quiche (keeps for 3 days)
* The scalloped potatoes (keeps for 3 days)
* The sections, zest, and juice of the organic oranges
* The sections and juice of the blood oranges
* The roasted squash, in its gratin dish (keeps for 4 days)

* The julienned carrots and the remaining broccoli (keeps for 1 week)
* The sliced onion with the garlic and ginger (keeps for 1 week)
* The chopped shallot and garlic (keeps for 1 week)
* The honey–soy sauce mixture (keeps for 1 week)
* The parsley (keeps for 1 week)

LEAVING SITTING OUT:

* The chopped toasted hazelnuts

Nothing requires freezing for this menu!

EACH NIGHT'S PREP

MONDAY

Appetizer: Celery root and parsnip velouté soup with scallops

Main: Crustless goat cheese and broccoli quiche

Reheating time: 10 minutes

Cooking time: 1 minute

Preparation time: 1 minute

Ingredients: the celery root and parsnip velouté soup, olive oil, one-fourth of the scallops (about 4 oz/113 g), curry powder, 4 sprigs of parsley, the crust-free quiche, salt

Preheat the oven to 325°F (160°C). Reheat the quiche for 10 minutes.

Meanwhile, reheat the velouté soup in its saucepan over low heat. When the soup is warm, heat 1 tbsp (15 mL) of olive oil in a small skillet. Cook the scallops over high heat for 30 seconds on each side. Season lightly with salt, and sprinkle them with 1 pinch of curry powder. Divide the scallops among individual bowls of the soup. Top with a little chopped parsley.

TUESDAY

Main: Duck breast à l'orange, scalloped potatoes

Reheating time: 10 minutes

Cooking time: 10 minutes

Preparation time: 5 minutes

Ingredients: the scalloped potatoes, the duck breasts, the quatre épices spice blend, the container with the organic orange sections, zest, and juice, half the quantity of the honey–soy sauce mixture

Preheat the oven to 325°F (160°C), and reheat the potatoes for 10 minutes.

Meanwhile, make 4 incisions crosswise along each duck breast using the tip of a knife. Heat a large skillet without any added fat. Place the duck breasts skin side down, and let cook over high heat for 7 minutes. Pour out any excess fat from the skillet, then continue cooking for 3 minutes over medium heat. Add ½ tsp of the quatre épices spice blend to the skillet, then pour in the orange juice to deglaze the pan, and the half quantity of the honey–soy sauce mixture. Let boil for 30 seconds, then turn off the heat. Set aside 1 cooked duck breast for Thursday's recipe. Thinly slice the remaining 3 breasts, arrange them in a serving dish, and top them with the orange zest. Pour the sauce (while it's still very warm) over the top, and decorate with the orange sections.

MENU #3

13

WEDNESDAY

Appetizer: Chickpea and orange salad

Main: Roasted red kuri squash, quinoa, goat cheese, hazelnuts

Reheating time: 10 minutes

Preparation time: 3 minutes

Ingredients: the chickpeas, the sections and juice of the blood oranges, the ground cumin, olive oil, 10 sprigs of parsley, the roasted squash, the cooked quinoa, the remaining goat cheese, the toasted hazelnuts, salt, and pepper

Drain and rinse the chickpeas. Place them in a large bowl. Add the orange juice and sections, ½ tsp of cumin, 3 tbsp (45 mL) of olive oil, and salt and pepper. Chop the parsley and add it to the bowl. Stir to combine, and serve.

Preheat the oven to 350°F (180°C), and reheat the squash for 10 minutes. Reheat the quinoa in the microwave and top it with the diced squash and its juice. Dice the goat cheese, and distribute it and the toasted hazelnuts on top.

15

THURSDAY

Main: Duck and noodles Chinese stir-fry

Cooking time: 10 minutes

Preparation time: 5 minutes

Ingredients: the Chinese noodles, olive oil, the container with the onion, garlic, and ginger, the julienned carrots and the broccoli florets, the remaining duck breast, the bean sprouts, the remaining honey–soy sauce mixture

Very thinly slice the duck breast, and remove the fat. Place the Chinese noodles in a bowl with 8 cups (2 L) of very hot water for 4 minutes. Heat 3 tbsp (45 mL) of olive oil in a sauté pan. Add the sliced onion, garlic, ginger, julienned carrots, and broccoli florets. Let cook for 4 minutes over high heat, stirring frequently. Add the duck breast and bean sprouts to the pan. Let cook for 2 minutes. Add the drained Chinese noodles and the honey–soy sauce mixture. Stir to combine and serve.

FRIDAY

Main: Scallop spaghetti

Cooking time: 15 minutes

Preparation time: 5 minutes

Ingredients: the spaghetti noodles, olive oil, the shallots and garlic, the remaining frozen scallops, the white wine, the crème fraîche, the remaining parsley, salt, and pepper

Cook the spaghetti noodles in boiling water according to the package directions. Heat 1 tbsp (15 mL) of olive oil in a sauté pan until warm. Add the shallots and garlic, and ½ tsp of salt. Let cook for 3 minutes over low heat, then add the scallops, and let cook for 1 minute on each side over high heat. Set aside off the heat. Deglaze the pan with the wine, add the crème fraîche, and sprinkle with the chopped parsley. Add the spaghetti noodles and the reserved scallops. Stir to combine, season with salt and pepper, and serve.

MENU #4

SHOPPING CART MENU #4

SHOPPING LIST   MENU #4

FRUITS / VEGETABLES

* 10 carrots
* 2 turnips
* 1 kohlrabi (a type of cabbage)
* 3⅓ lb (1.5 kg) Roseval potatoes (or other similar waxy potato)
* 1 precooked beet
* 1 head oakleaf lettuce
* 1 bunch parsley
* 6 yellow onions
* 3 garlic cloves

PANTRY AND STAPLES

* 2 cups (14 oz/400 g) green lentils
* 1⅓ cups (9 oz/250 g) white rice
* 3 bay leaves
* Cornstarch
* Mustard
* Wine vinegar
* Olive oil
* Sunflower oil
* Salt, black pepper

MEAT / FISH

* 1⅓ lb (600 g) fresh whiting fish fillets
* 1¾ lb (800 g) slightly salted pork shoulder
* 1 smoked sausage
* 4 slices ham
* 5¼ oz (150 g) smoked lardons (thick-cut cubed bacon)
* 4 beef filets

COLD CASE

* 6 large eggs
* 3⅓ cups (800 mL) heavy cream
* 1 cup (4 oz/113 g) shredded Comté cheese
* 1 wheel Reblochon cheese (or other similar soft alpine cheese)
* 5¼ oz (150 g) Roquefort cheese (or other creamy blue cheese)

DRY AND CANNED GOODS

* 4 traditional brioche buns
* 8 thick slices white sandwich bread
* 1 preserved lemon
* Scant ½ cup (100 mL) white wine
* 1 tbsp (1/2 oz/12 g) drained capers
* 4 cornichons (gherkins)

MENUS

MONDAY
Salt pork in lentils

TUESDAY
Tartiflette and crudités

WEDNESDAY
Appetizer: Stuffed brioche buns

Main: Whiting fish meatballs with winter vegetables

THURSDAY
Appetizer: Warm lentil salad, gribiche sauce

Main: Beef tenderloin, Roquefort cheese sauce

FRIDAY
Croque monsieur

SET UP

If you have enough work space, set out all the ingredients needed for this cooking session. This includes everything except the beet, ham, beef filets, 4 eggs, Comté, rice, white sandwich bread, capers, cornichons, and sunflower oil. This allows you to have everything at your fingertips and to not lose time searching for the ingredients in the pantry or refrigerator.

SET OUT THE NECESSARY EQUIPMENT:

* 1 lidded Dutch oven or small stockpot
* 1 large stockpot (or very large saucepan)
* 1 small saucepan
* 2 large saucepans
* 2 large bowls
* 1 small bowl
* 1 skillet
* 1 baking dish (for the tartiflette)
* 1 food processor
* 1 salad spinner (or clean kitchen towel)

* 7 containers: 3 large + 2 medium + 2 small
* Paper towels, parchment paper, airtight storage bag

EVERYTHING IS NOW READY FOR A COOKING TIME OF 2 HOURS AND 5 MINUTES!

1. Thoroughly rinse the pork shoulder under cold water to remove excess salt. Soak it for 5 minutes in a large bowl filled with cold water.

2. Peel all of the onions. Set aside 1 whole onion, then finely chop the remaining onions. Set the chopped onions aside in a large bowl.

3. Place the pork shoulder in the large stockpot, and cover it with cold water. Add the whole onion and 2 bay leaves. Bring to a boil, skim off any fat from the surface, and let cook for 1 hour and 30 minutes.

4. Meanwhile, place the lardons and 3 tbsp of the chopped onions in the skillet without any added fat. Cook for 10 minutes over medium heat.

5. Preheat the oven to 350°F (180°C). Peel and finely chop the garlic cloves. Place them in the small bowl.

6. Prepare the tartiflette: Peel the potatoes, and cut them into thin rounds. In the baking dish, arrange half the potato rounds, and add ½ tsp of the garlic, and the onion-lardons mixture. Top with the remaining potato rounds, then pour in about ¼ cup (60 mL) of white wine, 1¼ cups (300 mL) of cream, and season generously with salt and pepper. Cut the Reblochon wheel crosswise in half, and place the halves in the center of the baking dish lying flat. Bake for 50 minutes, or until golden and the cheese has melted.

7. In the Dutch oven, heat 2 tbsp (30 mL) of olive oil until warm. Add the remaining onions, half the garlic, and 1 tsp of salt. Let cook for 10 minutes over low heat.

8. Peel the carrots. Cut 8 of the carrots into rounds, and 2 into julienne (thin matchstick strips).

9. Pour the remaining wine into the pot, and let cook until the wine has evaporated. Add the carrot rounds, and 1 cup (240 mL) of water.

10. Peel the turnips and kohlrabi. Cut all the turnips and half the kohlrabi into cubes, and the remaining kohlrabi into julienne. Add the cubed vegetables to the pot in a single layer, and let cook for 20 minutes without stirring. Place the julienned kohlrabi in an airtight container with the julienned carrots.

11. Add the smoked sausage to the pot containing the pork shoulder.

12. In a large saucepan, bring water (not salted) to a boil. Rinse the lentils. Cook them for 20 minutes in the boiling water with 1 bay leaf.

13. Slice off the top of each brioche bun, then pull out the interior crumb (creating a bread bowl); set aside. Seal the hollow brioche shells inside the airtight storage bag, and set them in the refrigerator.

14. Wash the parsley, and gently dry it in the salad spinner (or with a clean kitchen towel). Repeat

these same steps with the lettuce. Place the parsley and lettuce in separate airtight containers between two sheets of paper towels.

15. Prepare the whiting fish meatballs: Remove the bones from the fish fillets. In the food processor, place the reserved brioche crumb, the fish fillets, the pulp from half the preserved lemon, ½ tsp of garlic, 2 sprigs of parsley, and some salt and pepper. Pulse to combine, just until the mixture comes together to form a ball. Shape the mixture into meatballs using the palms of your hands.

16. Remove the turnips and kohlrabi cubes and several carrot rounds from the pot, and place them in a large saucepan. Add a ladle of the cooking juices, and half the remaining preserved lemon. Place the meatballs on top, cover, and let cook for 10 minutes.

17. Drain the lentils. Add half the lentils to the pot with the carrots. Add the pork shoulder and the cooked sausage (cut into pieces) to the pot with 1 ladle of the cooking juices. Let cook 10 minutes.

Set aside the remaining cooked lentils in a medium-size container.

18. Prepare the Roquefort sauce: In the small saucepan, heat the Roquefort (diced) over low heat. Add a scant ½ cup (100 mL) of the cream and the remaining garlic. Bring to a boil, then lower the heat. Add 1 tbsp (⅓ oz/10 g) of cornstarch, and season generously with salt and pepper. Transfer the sauce to an airtight container. Wash the saucepan.

19. Fill the small saucepan with water and bring it to a boil. Add 2 eggs and cook them for 10 minutes.

20. Prepare the vinaigrette: Combine 2 tbsp (30 g) of mustard, 3 tbsp (45 mL) of vinegar, 1 tsp of salt, and a little pepper. Whisk vigorously while adding 6 tbsp (90 mL) of olive oil a little at a time.

IT'S ALL DONE! LET COOL.

PLACE IN THE REFRIGERATOR:

* The salt pork in lentils, in its pot (keeps for 2 days)
* The tartiflette (keeps for 3 days)
* The brioche buns in the airtight storage bag (keeps for 4 days)
* The cooked lentils (keeps for 5 days)
* The hard-boiled eggs (keeps for 5 days)
* The rinsed lettuce (keeps for 1 week)
* The vegetable sticks (keeps for 1 week)
* The washed parsley (keeps for 1 week)
* The vinaigrette (keeps for 1 week)

PLACE IN THE FREEZER:

* The beef filets, if you have purchased them from a butcher or if their sell-by date is less than 5 days
* The Roquefort sauce
* The whiting fish meatballs with the winter vegetables

EACH NIGHT'S PREP

MONDAY

Main: Salt pork in lentils

Reheating time: 15 minutes

Ingredients: the salt pork in lentils, 4 sprigs of parsley

Reheat the salt pork in lentils for 15 minutes over medium heat. Just before serving, chop the parsley and sprinkle it over the pork.

TUESDAY

Main: Tartiflette and crudités

Reheating time: 10 minutes

Preparation time: 2 minutes

Ingredients: the tartiflette, half the washed lettuce, the vegetable sticks, half the vinaigrette

Preheat the oven to 350°F (180°C), and reheat the tartiflette for 10 minutes.

In a large bowl, serve the lettuce with the vegetable sticks and the vinaigrette.

For Wednesday, remove the meatballs from the freezer and thaw them in the refrigerator.

WEDNESDAY

Appetizer: Stuffed brioche buns

Main: Whiting fish meatballs with winter vegetables

Reheating time: 15 minutes

Cooking time: 10 minutes

Preparation time: 10 minutes

Ingredients: the remaining 4 eggs, the hollow brioche buns, just over ¾ cup (200 mL) of cream, one-third of the Comté, 4 parsley sprigs, 4 lettuce leaves, the vinaigrette, the rice, the thawed meatballs, salt, and pepper

Preheat the oven to 400°F (200°C). Break 1 egg into each hollow brioche, add 1 tsp (5 mL) of cream, top with Comté, and season with salt, pepper, and parsley. Set the buns in a baking dish, and bake for 10 minutes. Serve with a small salad and some vinaigrette (reserving some of the vinaigrette for Friday). Cook the rice according to the package directions. Reheat the meatballs in a saucepan for 10 minutes. Add the remaining cream, then continue reheating for 5 more minutes. Serve with the rice.

For Thursday, remove the Roquefort cheese sauce from the freezer and the beef filets, if you have frozen them, and thaw in the refrigerator.

MENU #4

THURSDAY

Appetizer: Warm lentil salad, gribiche sauce

Main: Beef tenderloin, Roquefort cheese sauce

Reheating time: 10 minutes

Cooking time: 8 minutes

Preparation time: 10 minutes

Ingredients: the cooked lentils, the cornichons, half the remaining parsley, the hard-boiled eggs, 2 tbsp (30 g) of mustard, 3 tbsp (45 mL) of sunflower oil, 1 tbsp (15 mL) of wine vinegar, the capers, the thawed Roquefort cheese sauce, the beef filets, salt, and pepper

Gently reheat the lentils in the microwave. Finely chop the cornichons and parsley. Peel the hard-boiled eggs, cut them in half, and remove the yolks. Cut the whites into small dice.

Make a gribiche sauce: Crumble the yolks into a large bowl and add the mustard and some salt and pepper; stir to combine. Slowly drizzle in the sunflower oil while whisking to combine. Stir in the vinegar, capers, diced egg whites, and the chopped cornichons and parsley. Serve the warm lentils combined with the gribiche sauce.

In a small saucepan, reheat the Roquefort cheese sauce for 10 minutes over low heat. In a skillet, cook the beef filets for about 4 minutes on each side, more or less according to your preference. Season with salt and pepper, and serve with the sauce.

FRIDAY

Main: Croque monsieur

Cooking time: 10 minutes

Preparation time: 10 minutes

Ingredients: just over ¾ cup (200 mL) of cream, the remaining shredded Comté, the 8 slices of sandwich bread, the ham, the cooked beet, the remaining lettuce, the remaining vinaigrette, the remaining parsley, salt, and pepper

Preheat the oven to 400°F (200°C). In a bowl, combine the cream with half the remaining Comté, ½ tsp of salt, and a little pepper. On top of 1 slice of bread, place a folded piece of ham, sprinkle with 1 handful of shredded Comté, and top with a second slice of bread. Spread 1 tbsp of the Comté-cream mixture on top, and place the sandwich on a parchment-lined baking sheet. Repeat these steps with the remaining bread slices. Bake the croque monsieur for 10 minutes. Cut the beet into rounds, and serve on top of the lettuce with the vinaigrette, and a sprinkle of chopped parsley.

Acknowledgments

Thanks to Marin Postel, my editor, for her kindness, availability, and professionalism.

Thanks to Céline Le Lamer, Editorial Manager, for her trust and intelligence.

Thanks to Charly Deslandes, my photographer, for his perfect photos, his positive outlook, and his incredible efficacy.

Thanks to the Le Creuset brand for the Dutch ovens of exceptional quality, which I recommend to everyone; the investment is well worth it. An equal amount of thanks to the brand Greenpan for the ceramic cookware used in this book: skillets, sauté pans, woks, etc. To try them is to want to use them always!

Thanks to my local markets and supermarkets for their fresh products: fresh grocer Ben Saïd, fishmonger Forestier, Butcher Stéphane, Charcuterie Le Bon, Miele Primeur (Sandra), Roufia, and the team from my local La Vie Claire store.

Thanks to my family for their support: my mom (aka Mami Mumu), Benoit, Alexandre, Fred, and Eliott.

And thanks to all my friends who served as testers for the menus and recipes in this book: Caroline, Sakho, JB, Delphine, Florence, and Audrey.

Caroline Pessin

All the photographs in this book were taken by photographer Charly Deslandes.

Copyright © 2018 Hachette Livre (Hachette Pratique)

English translation copyright © 2019 by Black Dog & Leventhal Publishers

Cover design by Katie Benezra

Production design by Clea Chmela

Cover copyright © 2019 Hachette Book Group, Inc.

Hachette Book Group supports the right to free expression and the value of copyright. The purpose of copyright is to encourage writers and artists to produce the creative works that enrich our culture.

The scanning, uploading, and distribution of this book without permission is a theft of the author's intellectual property. If you would like permission to use material from the book (other than for review purposes), please contact permissions@hbgusa.com. Thank you for your support of the author's rights.

Black Dog & Leventhal Publishers
Hachette Book Group
1290 Avenue of the Americas
New York, NY 10104
www.hachettebookgroup.com
www.blackdogandleventhal.com

Originally published as *En Deux Heures, Je Cuisine Pour Toute la Semaine* in 2018 by Hachette Livre in France

First U.S. Edition: September 2019

Black Dog & Leventhal Publishers is an imprint of Perseus Books, LLC, a subsidiary of Hachette Book Group, Inc. The Black Dog & Leventhal Publishers name and logo are trademarks of Hachette Book Group, Inc.
The publisher is not responsible for websites (or their content) that are not owned by the publisher.
The Hachette Speakers Bureau provides a wide range of authors for speaking events. To find out more, go to www.HachetteSpeakersBureau.com or call (866) 376-6591.

ISBNs: 978-0-7624-9508-5 (paper over board); 978-0-7624-9509-2 (ebook)

Library of Congress Control Number: 2018966390

Printed in China

IM

10 9 8 7 6 5 4 3 2 1